D0792989

# TREKKING IN
# THE ZILLERTAL ALPS

## About the Author

Allan has been passionate about mountains and photography since his early teens. He has climbed extensively throughout the Alps, discovering Austria by chance many years ago while trying to avoid atrocious weather conditions in the higher mountains of the Western Alps. He believes Austria remains one of mountaineering's best kept secrets, better suited to the average mountaineer than the higher mountains to the west.

In addition to Austria and the Alps, Allan has climbed from East Africa to the Falkland Islands, the Greater Ranges of Nepal and Pakistan, the Zagros Mountains of Iran and the Al Hajr mountains of the Arabian Peninsula. A long-standing member of the Austrian Alpine Club (UK), Sektion Britannia, he is also a member of the Outdoor Writers and Photographers Guild, an Associate of the Royal Photographic Society and a holder of the International Mountain Leaders Award. His home is on the edge of the Yorkshire Dales. For more about Allan, visit www.allanhartley.co.uk.

### Other Cicerone guides by the author
*Trekking in Austria's Hohe Tauern*
*Trekking in the Alps* (contributing author)
*Trekking in the Stubai Alps*

# TREKKING IN THE ZILLERTAL ALPS

by Allan Hartley

2 POLICE SQUARE, MILNTHORPE, CUMBRIA LA7 7PY
www.cicerone.co.uk

Second edition 2013
ISBN-13: 978 1 85284 717 3
First edition 2003
ISBN-13: 978 1 85284 370 0
Printed in China on behalf of Latitude Press Ltd
A catalogue record for this book is available from the British Library.
All photographs are by the author unless otherwise stated.

## Acknowledgements

To the many members of the Austrian Alpine Club (UK) who have accompanied me over several decades visiting the Zillertal, particularly my wife Marilyn and daughter Zoe, the late Helmut Meier, Robert Hampson, the Jays, Ken and Christine Talbot, Alan Nuttall, Mike Garrett, Rob Stevenson, Martin Haydon, Wilf Bishop, Ray Johnson, Terry O'Donnell, Jim Cox, Len Reilly, Sarah Phillips, Ged O'Neill, American cousin Mike Macken and finally evergreen Kiwi Doug Ball.

This book is dedicated to Helmut Meier, friend and companion on many an alpine journey, who was killed in a tragic accident while descending from the Dristner in the Zillertal.

## Advice to Readers

While every effort is made by our authors to ensure the accuracy of guidebooks as they go to print, changes can occur during the lifetime of an edition. If we know of any, there will be an Updates tab on this book's page on the Cicerone website (www.cicerone.co.uk), so please check before planning your trip. We also advise that you check information about such things as transport, accommodation and shops locally. Even rights of way can be altered over time. We are always grateful for information about any discrepancies between a guidebook and the facts on the ground, sent by email to info@cicerone.co.uk or by post to Cicerone, 2 Police Square, Milnthorpe LA7 7PY, United Kingdom.

*Front cover:* Above Friesenberg Haus with the Hochfeiler in the distance

# CONTENTS

## Warning

Mountain walking can be a dangerous activity carrying a risk of personal injury or death. It should be undertaken only by those with a full understanding of the risks and with the training and experience to evaluate them. While every care and effort has been taken in the preparation of this guide, the user should be aware that conditions can be highly variable and can change quickly, materially affecting the seriousness of a mountain walk. Therefore, except for any liability which cannot be excluded by law, neither Cicerone nor the author accept liability for damage of any nature (including damage to property, personal injury or death) arising directly or indirectly from the information in this book.

To call out the Mountain Rescue, ring the international emergency number 112: this will connect you via any available network. Once connected to the emergency operator, ask for the police.

# Map Key

|  |  |
|---|---|
| ～ | ridge |
| ▭ | water/lake |
| ⋯⌢⋯ | trek or ascent route |
| ▲ ⬦ | staffed/unstaffed mountain hut |
| ■ | other building |
| ⬦ | settlement |
| ∿∿∿ | road |
| ? | hazard, eg loose ground, crevasses |
| ⅄ | col |
| ▲ | summit cairn |
| ⚑SP | signpost |
| **R100** | route number |
| **4** | stage number |
| † | summit cross |
| B | bridge |
| * | viewpoint |
| 🌲 | forest |
| FR | fixed ropes |
| Ⓗ | bus stop |
| ▭▭▭ | ladder |
| ⎯ ⎯ ⎯ | international border |
| ▨ | glacier |

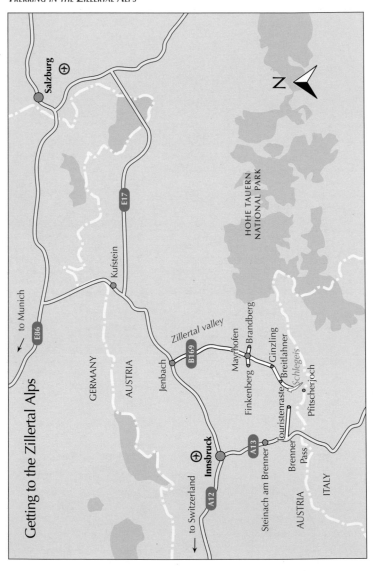

Getting to the Zillertal Alps

# Zillertal Alps from the North

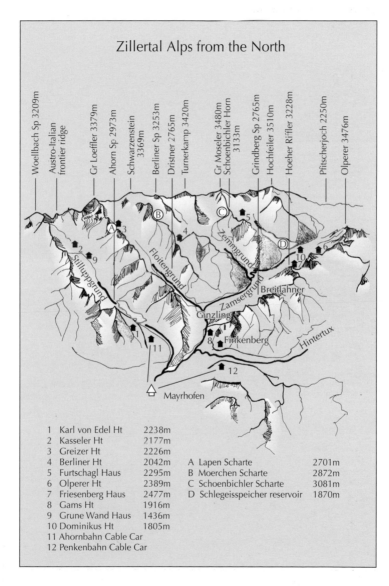

Woellbach Sp 3209m
Austro-Italian frontier ridge
Gr Loeffler 3379m
Ahorn Sp 2973m
Schwarzenstein 3369m
Berliner Sp 3253m
Dristner 2765m
Turnerkamp 3420m
Gr Moseler 3480m
Schoenbichler Horn 3133m
Grindberg Sp 2765m
Hochfeiler 3510m
Hoeher Rifler 3228m
Pfitscherjoch 2250m
Olperer 3476m

Stillupgrund
Floitengrund
Zemmgrund
Zamsergrund
Breitlahner
Ginzling
Finkenberg
Hintertux
Mayrhofen

| | | |
|---|---|---|
| 1  Karl von Edel Ht | 2238m | |
| 2  Kasseler Ht | 2177m | |
| 3  Greizer Ht | 2226m | |
| 4  Berliner Ht | 2042m | |
| 5  Furtschagl Haus | 2295m | A  Lapen Scharte | 2701m |
| 6  Olperer Ht | 2389m | B  Moerchen Scharte | 2872m |
| 7  Friesenberg Haus | 2477m | C  Schoenbichler Scharte | 3081m |
| 8  Gams Ht | 1916m | D  Schlegeisspeicher reservoir | 1870m |
| 9  Grune Wand Haus | 1436m | |
| 10 Dominikus Ht | 1805m | |
| 11 Ahornbahn Cable Car | | |
| 12 Penkenbahn Cable Car | | |

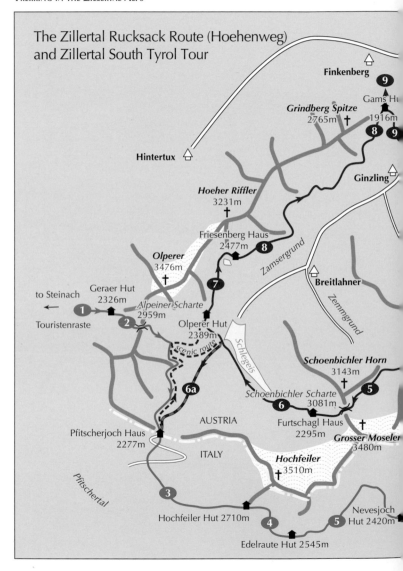

The Zillertal Rucksack Route (Hoehenweg)
and Zillertal South Tyrol Tour

Finkenberg
**9**

Gams Hut

*Grindberg Spitze*
2765m †
1916m
**8** **9**

Hintertux

Ginzling

*Hoeher Riffler*
3231m
†

Friesenberg Haus
2477m **8**

Zamsergrund

*Olperer*
3476m
†

Breitlahner

Zemmgrund

to Steinach ←
Geraer Hut
2326m
*Alpeiner Scharte*
2959m
**7**

Touristenraste
**1**
**2**

Olperer Hut
2389m
*scenic route*

Schlegeis

*Schoenbichler Horn*
3143m
†
**5**

**6a**

*Schoenbichler Scharte*
3081m
**6**

Furtschagl Haus
2295m
†

Pfitscherjoch Haus
2277m

AUSTRIA

*Grosser Moseler*
3480m

ITALY

*Hochfeiler*
†3510m

*Pfitschertal*

**3**

Nevesjoch
Hut 2420m

Hochfeiler Hut 2710m
**4**
**5**

Edelraute Hut 2545m

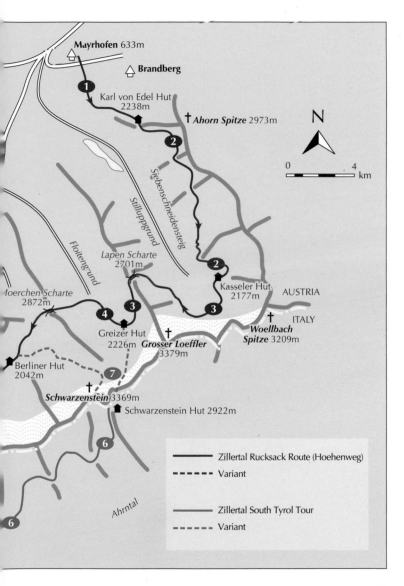

Mayrhofen 633m

△ Brandberg

**1**

Karl von Edel Hut
2238m

† *Ahorn Spitze* 2973m

N

0    4 km

Siebenschneidensteig

Stilluppgrund

**2**

Floitengrund

Lapen Scharte
2701m

**2**

Kasseler Hut
2177m

AUSTRIA

Moerchen Scharte
2872m

**3**

**4**

**3**

ITALY

Greizer Hut
2226m

† *Grosser Loeffler*
3379m

*Woellbach
Spitze* 3209m

† Berliner Hut
2042m

**7**

† *Schwarzenstein* 3369m

▲ Schwarzenstein Hut 2922m

**6**

—————  Zillertal Rucksack Route (Hoehenweg)

- - - - -  Variant

Ahrntal

—————  Zillertal South Tyrol Tour

- - - - -  Variant

**6**

*Approaching the summit of the Hoeher Riffler (ZRR Stage 7), looking southwest to the Friesenberg Scharte and Gefrorne Wand Spitze, with the pyramid wedge of the Olperer (right) and Fusstein (left) in the distance*

# INTRODUCTION

In the heart of the pristine Austrian Tyrol rise the shapely, snow-capped peaks of the Zillertal Alps. Dotted with top-quality huts connected by clear paths, they offer a premier trekking region for novices and for experts.

To the east, the Zillertal merges with the mountains of the Reichen and Venediger Groups and the province of Ost (East) Tyrol; to the west is the Brenner Pass into Italy and the mountains of the Stubai Alps. Southwards are Italy and the South Tyrol, along with the mountains at the head of the Zillertal valley which, together with its huts, was annexed to Italy at the end of the First World War. To the north is the Inn valley, which runs the entire length of the Tyrol. The Zillertal is the longest subsidiary valley in the Tyrol at some 50km long, and terminates at the picturesque and popular holiday resort town of Mayrhofen.

Above Mayrhofen the main Zillertal valley splits off into a number of subsidiary valleys, and they in turn also branch off in various directions. To the east is the steeply sided Zillergrund valley, flanked by the Ahorn Spitze and Brandberg Kolm, with the village of Brandberg and farming hamlets of Inder Au and Barenbad leading to the Zillergrund reservoir and the old cattle drovers' trail into the Ahrntal valley of Italy and the South Tyrol.

To the west are the villages of Finkenberg and Hintertux and the mountains of the Tuxer Hauptkamm and the Hintertux valley, flanked by the peaks of the Grindberg Spitze to the south and Tuxer Alpen to the north, with the Penkenjoch and Rastkogel. To the southwest is the main Zamsergrund valley and the delightful village of Ginzling and hamlet of Breitlahner, beyond which the road terminates at the head of the Zamsergrund valley by the Schlegeisspeicher hydro-electric reservoir and the ancient trade route into the Pfitschertal valley of Italy and the South Tyrol via Pfitscherjoch.

Immediately to the south of Mayrhofen are the peaks of the Ahorn Spitze, Dristner and the bulk of the Grindberg Spitze – all stand tall and are unmissable from the railway station. Above the tree line the horizon to the south is dominated by the peaks sharing the border with Italy and the South Tyrol, particularly the Hochfeiler, Grosser Moseler and Schwarzenstein, profiles that will become familiar features of your trek.

## THE RUCKSACK ROUTE AND SOUTH TYROL TOUR

The **Zillertal Rucksack Route** (ZRR), also known as the Berliner Hoehenweg (German) or Zillertaler Runde Tour (Austrian), is a hut-to-hut tour that

13

*Ascent of the Ahorn Spitze on the track just above the Edel Hut (end of ZRR Stage 1)*

starts above Mayrhofen from the Karl von Edel Hut and then visits each of the following huts in turn, Kasseler, Greizer, Berliner, Furtschagl Haus, Olperer, Friesenberg Haus to end at the Gams Hut high above the charming village of Ginzling before returning to Mayrhofen. This gives a continuous walk of about ten days, which can be extended to include ascents of the local peaks, Klettersteige rock scramble adventures (on via ferrata-type protected routes), and even rest days. The length of the tour is 70–80km, depending on where you start and finish, and it ascends some 6700m.

As the name suggests, the Rucksack Route can be traversed entirely without crossing glaciers and without specialist climbing skills. However, it does involve negotiating steep ground, crossing late summer snow and making use of fixed wire ropes here and there that are installed to aid stability. To climb some of the peaks described in the 'Excursion' sections of the guide, it is necessary to make glacier crossings, for which the required skills and kit are essential (see 'Alpine walking skills and equipment' below).

The **Zillertal South Tyrol Tour** (ZSTT) is virtually unknown outside the South Tyrol, which is one of the key ingredients that helps to make it interesting and different. The tour starts from the Bergbauernhof farmstead at Touristenraste, not far from the small industrial town of Steinach am Brenner. From Touristenraste the it first progresses to the Geraer Hut, and then enters the Zillertal and South

Tyrol proper at Pfitscherjoch Haus on the border with Italy. (Conveniently, Pfitscherjoch Haus also provides an alternative starting point for those wishing to join the tour from Mayrhofen and the Zillertal valley.) From Pfitscherjoch Haus the tour heads for the historic Hochfeiler Hut, and continues by way of the Edelraute, Nevesjoch and Schwarzenstein Huts before returning to Austria across the Schwarzensteinkees or Floitenkees glaciers to either the Berliner or Greizer Hut. From both huts, there is access to Mayrhofen and onward transport.

Excluding the peaks, this gives a continuous hut-to-hut tour of eight days, with good opportunities along the way to climb the Hochfeiler and Grosser Moseler, two of the Zillertal's most prestigious mountains. Overall the tour is about 55km long and ascends just over 5000m (without considering climbing any peaks). It is physically demanding and will perhaps appeal to more experienced alpine walkers who wish to undertake a tour that is more remote and challenging.

The Zillertal's highest peak is the Hochfeiler (3510m), and there are a further 40 peaks over 3000m, many of which are glaciated or have permanent snow cover. The Zillertal arena provides ample opportunity for all mountain enthusiasts. It is ideal for first-time visitors to the Alps (with the ZRR being particularly suitable for capable family groups with children) and for aspiring alpinists.

However, it should be remembered that the Zillertal is not necessarily a tame area in comparison with the Western Alps, as these mountains can challenge even the most experienced. Whatever your aspirations, you will not be disappointed.

*Gruss Gott und sehr gut Zillerbergtouren.*

## WHEN TO GO

The summer season usually starts in mid-June, when the huts open, and ends in late September, when the huts close. During this time the paths and passes are relatively free of snow.

June is early season and not the best time to visit, as it is not unusual to come across large amounts of old snow lying on north-facing slopes, such as those of the Lapen Scharte.

In July, the weather is warmer and the winter snow further recedes, although there are more people in the mountains and at the huts.

August is seen as the peak season when most Europeans take their holidays. The huts are at their busiest. The weather is at its most settled, although it is not unusual to see cloud build up late in the mornings and thunderstorms in the evenings. August is when most of the villages in the Zillertal hold their summer church festivals known as Kirchtags. They are extremely good fun, and it is well worth a visit to villages such as Stumm and Finkenberg, where the village will be set up with market stalls,

*The Hochfeiler (3510m), highest peak in the Zillertal (end of STT Stage 3)*

street entertainment, local crafts and lots of music for a good day out, to be thoroughly enjoyed by all.

September announces the onset of autumn. The weather will be cooler and the huts quieter as they head towards the end of the season.

For a two-week holiday, the middle of July or the first two weeks in September are recommended.

## GETTING THERE

Getting to Austria is relatively straightforward no matter how you decide to travel. For the ZRR your first point of contact with the Zillertal valley is at the major road and railway intersection at the industrial town of Jenbach, in the Inn valley. Thereafter, the 50km (30-mile), 1hr journey up the Zillertal

valley by road or rail leads to the resort town of Mayrhofen, the starting point of the ZRR (and the alternative start point for the ZSTT). Those undertaking the ZSTT need to head to Innsbruck, the provincial capital of Tyrol, before continuing by regional train to the small town of Steinach am Brenner, near the start point of the tour. (See Appendix C for a glossary of useful German–English travel words and phrases.)

### By air (and rail)
Even if you travel by air, which is the quickest way to get to Austria and the Zillertal, for those undertaking the ZRR there is not always sufficient time to leave the United Kingdom in the early morning, catch a train to Jenbach and Mayrhofen, and then travel on to

one of the huts before nightfall. It is better to stay overnight in Mayrhofen and then continue your journey the day after. However, if you are travelling light and have no hold-ups, it is just about possible to get to the Edel Hut by early evening. Similarly, for those undertaking the ZSTT it is better to stay overnight in Innsbruck or Steinach am Brenner.

Munich is the main entry point (from London, Manchester, Birmingham), but flights also go to Salzburg and Innsbruck (from London). Some of the major operators, particularly Lufthansa, have several flights a day from London, Manchester and Birmingham. Other budget carriers also operate from Luton, Gatwick and Stansted. (See Appendix B for airline websites.)

Although travelling by air gets you to mainland Europe quickly, you may lose precious time transferring to the railway station, the Hauptbahnhof, and may experience frustrating delays and hold-ups just finding your way about.

At **Munich**, the airport connects direct with the regional railway network, where there are frequent trains every 30mins or so. Follow the train signs DB and S. You need a pre-paid ticket before getting on the train. Do not push your luck without a ticket, as the Germans do not take kindly to freeloaders no matter where they come from. Be warned. There is a railway booking office in the airport arrivals hall adjacent to the concession counters for car hire, hotel reservations and so on. This facility is not always open, but if it is get your ticket to Jenbach *hin und zuruck* (there and back) if you are coming back the same way. There are frequent express trains every 2hrs or so. Once on your journey, get off the regional train at Munchen Ost (Munich East), listen to the announcements, and change platforms to get on one of the inter-city trains (*schnell zug*). Look out for the matrix sign boards at the station and on the side of the train, and get on the first one that has Innsbruck on it or Brennero, Venezia or Venedig – anything heading into Italy or Switzerland will do, as they all have to go via Jenbach.

If the ticket office is closed at Munich airport you can get your ticket at Munich East – the ticket office is at road level with other shops and fast food outlets. With express trains it is also possible to pay on the train, sometimes at a premium, if you can show that you had to rush and didn't have enough time to get to the ticket office.

Railway tickets may also be purchased in advance and online by visiting www.bahn.de. There is a thumbnail Union Flag icon for English speakers to click.

At **Jenbach**, there is a local bus service and a narrow-gauge railway to the roadhead at Mayrhofen. This journey takes about 1hr. The last train to Mayrhofen is at 19.44, and the last bus at 21.08.

*Mayrhofen Bahnhof railway station, with Dampfzug Puffing Billy train and the Ahorn Spitze on the left-hand skyline*

Jenbach is the home of the Zillertal railway and its collection of old steam locomotives, known as the Dampfzug. But, more famed as Thomas the Tank Engine or simply Puffing Billy, these charming little trains are every kid's delight. One of these little trains travels up and down the Zillertal valley throughout the season, pulling behind it 100-year-old bright red carriages. If you have children with you, the Dampfzug is a fitting way to start or end your journey in the Zillertal. There are only two Dampfzug trains per day, and many of the seats are reserved in advance, so plan your journey well (Jenbach/Mayrhofen 10.32/15.16; Mayrhofen/Jenbach 13.06/17.06).

At **Salzburg**, take Line 2 bus service from the airport to the Hauptbahnhof, from where a rail ticket can be purchased to Jenbach or Innsbruck. Journey time is just over 1hr, travelling west along the Inn valley.

At **Innsbruck**, from the airport there are a bus service and taxis to Innsbruck city centre and the

Hauptbahnhof main railway station. Then take the regional train service to Jenbach or Steinach am Brenner.

## By rail

Consult with Eurostar, but the two most commonly used routes are as follows. Each route gets travellers to Innsbruck and Jenbach within 18hrs of leaving London.

- London–Dover–Calais–Paris–Zurich–Innsbruck–Jenbach
- London–Dover–Ostend–Brussels–Munich–Jenbach

Check these websites for further details.

- German Railways DB (Deutsche Bundesbahn), www.bahn.de
- Austrian Railways OBB (Osterreichische Bundesbahnen), www.oebb.at
- Verkehrsverbund Tirol, www.vvt.at
- Post bus, www.postbus.at
- Zillertal railway, www.zillertalbahn.at

## By road

The most direct route by road is via the Dover–Ostend channel crossing, then by the motorway system to Munich and into Austria at Kufstein, followed by the short drive up the Inn valley to Jenbach and Mayrhofen. An alternative route goes from Dover by Lille to Luxembourg, then to Saarbrucken, Pirmasens, Bad Bergzabern, Karlsruhl, Stuttgart, Munich, Kufstein, Jenbach and Mayrhofen.

With more than one driver it is just about possible to get to Mayrhofen within 24hrs from Calais or Ostend. Whatever your chosen route, consult with your motoring organisation before setting out.

It is also important, when parking your car, to consider the return journey and getting back to it, as this is not always easy if you are forced to drop down into another valley (more likely on the ZSTT). It may be best to leave your car in Innsbruck or Jenbach, or one of the other major villages that has good bus or railway connections to and from Mayrhofen.

The following motor organisation websites provide useful information – www.adac.de and www.oeamfc.at.

## GETTING BACK

For those travelling by air, the last day of your vacation needs to be devoted to making the journey home. The journey time from Mayrhofen to Munich airport is around 2½hrs, to Salzburg 2hr, and to Innsbruck 2hr.

- The first train from Mayrhofen to **Jenbach** is at 06.30, then there are services roughly every ½hr from 06.50 onwards.
- The earliest train from Jenbach to **Munich** is at 08.07, with services at 09.02 and 10.57. Remember to change trains at Munchen Ost and get on the regional shuttle-train service S8 marked 'Flughafen'.
- From Jenbach the train times to **Salzburg** are roughly every two hours – 09.26, 10.02 and 11.26.

## ACCOMMODATION IN THE VALLEY

There is no shortage of good places to stay in Mayrhofen and the Zillertal, as the whole district is geared to tourism and catering for visitors.

### Hotels

In Mayrhofen, the main centre of the Zillertal, hotels tend to cater for the tourist trade, and accommodation is more expensive here than in the surrounding villages, but there is an abundance of guest houses and small hotels in the area where climbers and walkers may feel more at home. If you are not bothered about nightlife, then there are good bargains in the villages of Fugen, Kaltenbach, Zell am Ziller and Ramsau. The Hotel Poste in Jenbach, and the same in Kaltenbach, is recommended. Anyone booking hut accommodation over the internet will find that many huts have family connections with guest houses and hotels in the valley, and they will be happy to make recommendations.

For those wishing to stay in Mayrhofen, the Siegelerhof Gastehof, opposite the conference centre and main Tourist Information Office, is within 5mins walk of the railway station. It is managed by the Hausberger family, who provide good, clean, inexpensive bed and breakfast accommodation (tel 0043 5285 62493 or 62424, email siegelerhof@tirol.com, www.hotel-siegelerhof.at).

For accommodation in Steinach am Brenner (for the ZSTT) and Salzburg, see Appendix B. Should you need to stay in Innsbruck, hotels can be booked from the tourist information centre at the railway station

*A typical street scene in Mayrhofen*

located on the lower ground floor of the ticket hall (see Appendix B for recommended places to stay in the area).

## Campsites
Those with a car will find good sites on the outskirts of Mayrhofen (camping Kroell, tel 0043 5285 62580), at Schlitters, Kaltenbach (camping Hochzillertal, tel 0043 6507 333398), Zell am Ziller (camping Hoffer, tel 0043 5282 2248) and Laubichl. See www.camping@alpenparadies.com. Groups intending to camp should enquire from the campsite warden about reduced fees while they are away. This is referred to as *leeres zelt*.

## Youth hostels
There is no youth hostel (Verein Volkshaus) in Mayrhofen. The nearest hostel is in Innsbruck, located some 15mins walk on the northern site of the River Inn (email jgh.volkshaus-ibk@aon.at, www.jgh.volkshaus-ibk.at; see Appendix B for more details).

## THE ZILLERTAL VALLEY AND MAYRHOFEN

From its entrance at Strass to its head at Mayrhofen, the 50km Zillertal valley is everything Tyrolean, with pretty chalet-style houses and organised charm. To the east the valley is bounded by the Kitzbuehler Alpen, while to the west are the lesser peaks of the Tuxer Alpen. Further up the valley lie the charming villages of Schlitters, Fugen-Hart, Kaltenbach-Stumm, Zell am Ziller, Hippach-Ramsau and lastly Mayrhofen – the Zillertal's main village-cum-town and commercial centre, with the main peaks of the Zillertal mountains at its head.

The delightful town of Mayrhofen is one of the main holiday resorts in the Tyrol, wholly geared up for summer and winter tourism to suit all tastes and budgets. However, development came late to Mayrhofen, as it is located some 50km up a dead-end valley in the middle of nowhere, isolated from the main communication links of the Inn valley. While the Romans showed interest, and various wandering tribes came and went, the problems of access for trade always made it difficult for settlements to establish themselves in the valley.

Named after a few farms at the head of the valley, Mayrhofen started to feature in rural affairs at the start of the 18th century, mainly in relation to farming and as a good place to hunt and collect minerals. This isolation was no defence during the Napolenic wars of 1809, and the Zillertal menfolk picked up their arms and opted to fight for Tyrolean independence against the French and Bavarians with the folklore hero Andreas Hofer. Sadly this fight was lost and resulted in the Tyrol being ruled by the Bavarians for the next few years. By 1816 Napoleon had been defeated. The Tyrol was handed back to its rightful owners, with all the provinces united under the Royal Household of Emperor Franz Joseph I.

With the war over, almost another 50 years would pass before tourism and mountain wandering became part of the local economy with the establishment of the Austrian Alpine Club (OeAV) in 1862 and the opening of the Berliner Hut in 1879. Construction of the railway in 1902, which was built initially to support forestry and the transportation of minerals and magnesite ore from the lucrative mines of Hintertux, opened up the Zillertal valley immensely. Since then Mayrhofen has grown steadily through the wealth created by the Zillertal valley from agriculture, farming and forestry – but above all through tourism.

## Activities for poor weather days

Mayrhofen, and the Zillertal in general, can be a rather miserable place should you be unfortunate enough to have indifferent weather, for the clouds just swirl around and refuse to budge from the peaks. Local lore has it that if the Ahorn Sptize has a raised hat, the weather will be good; if the hat is pulled down over his ears, the weather will be bad!

To help keep you entertained, particularly if you have children with you, here are some suggestions for what to do (other than the normal theme park activities) in poor weather.

**Rattenberg** This small, delightful medieval town with timber-framed quirky buildings and cobbled streets is famous for handmade glass. Take the train to Jenbach then the local bus service to Brixlegg and Rattenberg.

**Schwaz** (medieval silver mine) Take the train to Jenbach, then the regional train heading to Innsbruck, and get off at Schwaz; thereafter it's a short walk to the visitor centre (see www.silberbergwerk.at).

**Zillerbach River** (white-water rafting) Great in the rain when the Zillerbach river is in flood; reservation offices in Mayrhofen.

**Klettersteige** It needs to be dry, but anyone armed with climbing tackle may find some consolation in indifferent weather by trying the Klettersteige (via ferrata-type protected climbing routes) that start near Gasthof Zillertal, not far from Mayrhofen railway station on the west side of the river.

**Innsbruck** Capital city of the province of Tyrol, named after the river on which it stands, overlooked by the Karwendel group of mountains and made famous as a centre for winter Olympics sports. The city is well worth a visit in its own right – particularly for the Old City (Alte Stadt), but also for the OeAV Alpenvereins Museum (open Monday to Saturday during normal business hours). Located within the Hofburg Imperial Palace in the Old Town, it has many fine exhibits from alpinism's golden era, perhaps the most notable being memorabilia of Hermann Buehl's ascent of Nanga Parbat in the Karakoram mountains of Pakistan.

Take the train to Jenbach followed by the regional train to Innsbruck. It is a 10min walk from the railway station (Hauptbahnhof) to the Old City.

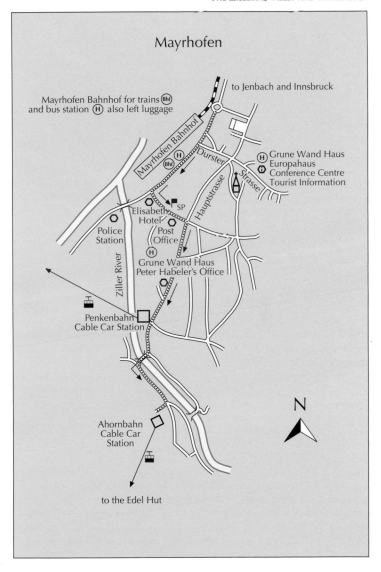

Mayrhofen

to Jenbach and Innsbruck

Mayrhofen Bahnhof for trains (Bhf)
and bus station (H) also left luggage

Mayrhofen Bahnhof

Durster

Grune Wand Haus
Europahaus
Conference Centre
Tourist Information

SP

Elisabeth
Hotel

Police
Station

Post
Office

Hauptstrasse

Strasse

Grune Wand Haus
Peter Habeler's Office

Ziller River

Penkenbahn
Cable Car Station

N

Ahornbahn
Cable Car
Station

to the Edel Hut

*Mayrhofen Haupt Strasse (high street)*

**Out and about in Mayrhofen**
See the street map (previous page) for the location of the railway and bus station, tourist information office and post office. Useful websites include www.mayrhofen.at and www.zillertal.at.

**Bus services**
The following times are for the local post bus service that leaves from Mayrhofen's combined train and bus station.
*Mayrhofen to Ginzling/Breitlahner/Schlegeis*
06.40/07.55/09.25/11.25/13.25/15.25/16.55/17.55

*Schlegeis to Mayrhofen*
09.35/10.35/13.55/15.35/16.35/17.55
*Breitlahner to Mayrhofen*
09.55/10.55/14.15/15.55/16.35/18.15
*Ginzling to Mayrhofen*
10.10/11.10/14.30/16.10/17.10/18.30

**Tourist offices**
The main tourist information office and conference centre, the Europahaus, is located near the railway station on Durster Strasse. There are also satellite tourist offices in the town (see Appendix B for full contact details).

**Post office and mail**

The post office in Mayrhofen is located just off the main street in the centre of town (see street map), and has fax, internet and money-exchange facilities. The post office is open Monday to Friday from 08.00 to 12.00, then 14.00 to 18.00.

At huts postcards can be purchased and mailed from the hut's post box. The mail is then taken down to the valley, usually once a week and deposited at the main post office. Not surprisingly, post to UK can take 10–20 days.

**Places to leave luggage**

There is a left-luggage facility at the combined bus and railway station, which is open Monday to Saturday 08.00 to 18.00. Alternatively, should you be staying at one of the hotels, most hoteliers are quite happy to store luggage until you return.

**Peter Habeler's office (mountain guides)**

The services of a professional mountain guide can be hired via Peter Habeler's office on Mayrhofen's main high street (Haupt Strasse). See Appendix B for more information or contact www.bergfuehrer-zillertal.at.

### TREKKING WITH CHILDREN

How suitable is hut-to-hut touring for children? The Austrian Alpine Club actively encourages children to participate in mountain activities, and most children love visiting the various huts and the sense of freedom it gives them. Children need to be fit, but if they are capable of ascending Ben Nevis, Snowdon or the round of Helvellyn then they will surely enjoy some of these tours. The author's daughter traversed the entire length of the ZRR and climbed several peaks along the way when she was 14 years old, and children as young as eight have undertaken the majority of the tour. However, the ZSTT is not really suitable for children under 15 years.

But only parents can decide, since some of the day's outings are quite long, particularly the Greizer to Berliner Hut and Berliner Hut to Furtschagl Haus stages. Children must be happy to be in the mountains for long periods at a time and easily entertained in the evenings, reading books, playing scrabble or simply

*A family from London trekking in the Zillertal with children aged 12 and 8, still smiling!*

chatting. One good tip is to have a friend with them for company and it is important to make sure that they have adequate stops en route and rest days.

## HEALTH AND FITNESS

While you do not have to be super-fit to undertake these tours, it is essential that participants are used to walking for 6hrs continuously while carrying a touring-size rucksack weighing in the region of 12–15kg.

### Altitude

The average altitude encountered on the tour is around 2500m–3000m (8000ft–10,000ft), so people visiting the Zillertal do not usually suffer badly from altitude sickness. However, you may feel the effects of altitude – such as feeling out of breath, mild headache and slowed pace – particularly on the high peaks such as the Grosser Moseler and Olperer. The best defence against altitude is to be as fit as possible, eat and drink normally, and to get adequate rest and sleep.

## EMERGENCIES AND MOUNTAIN SAFETY

Both the tours in this guide involve sustained activity in a mountain environment. Inevitably, this increases the risk of an accident taking place, such as a severe fall, a broken limb or some other serious mishap, which will all result in the mountain rescue team being called out.

One of the benefits of membership of the OeAV is mountain rescue insurance in case of accident. This can be supplemented from a specialist insurance company, details of which are available from the Austrian Alpine Club (UK) and the advertisement sections of one of the many climbing magazines. Similarly the British Mountaineering Council (BMC) has an excellent insurance policy, which can be obtained separately to membership.

The value of insurance should not be underestimated, as the cost of a mountain rescue can be considerable when helicopters, police and professional mountain guides are brought into use. Unlike in the United Kingdom, where mountain rescue services are generally provided free of charge by the local authority and mountain rescue teams run by enthusiastic volunteers, in the alpine regions most countries will charge the hapless victim. Be warned!

Mountain safety is as much about prevention as it is about cure, so check out all your gear, practise constructing your improvised rudimentary harness and the time-consuming tasks of putting on crampons/harnesses and roping up, and develop your glacier travel skills and crevasse rescue techniques before you go (see 'Alpine walking skills', below).

### European Health Insurance Card (EHIC)

This card (previously form E111) is available free from any post office

## EMERGENCIES

Emergency services operate on a different satellite frequency to normal services, so the following numbers can be dialled from a mobile phone even when the phone indicates that there is no reception from your service provider. Fortunately, in Austria mobile phone reception is excellent.

- Mountain Rescue (Bergrettung) Austria 140
- Mountain Rescue (Bergrettung) Italy 118
- Red Cross (Rotes Kreutz) 144
- European emergency telephone number 112

### International Alpine Distress Signal

*Help required*: signalled by shouting, blowing a whistle or flashing a torch at 10 second intervals for one minute. Then pause for one minute and repeat.
*Answer received*: signalled by shouting, a whistle or a flashing a torch at 20 second intervals. Then pause for one minute and repeat.

### Signals to helicopters

**Help required**
Raise both arms above head to form a 'Y'

**Help not required**
Raise one arm above head and extend the other downward, to form the diagonal of an 'N'

Should you be involved with a helicopter rescue...
- Stay at least 50m from the helicopter.
- Do not approach the helicopter unless signalled by the winch man to do so.
- Do not approach the helicopter from behind.
- Ensure that all loose items of equipment are made secure.

– just fill in the form to receive a credit-card-size EHIC identity card that entitles you to free medical care in any EU member state, including Austria. Should you be unfortunate enough to need medical attention while on holiday, then this card will help to pay your way. However, the EHIC entitles the holder only to those services provided free in the member

The Siebenschneidenweg ('seven ridges way'), as seen in profile from below the Lapen Scharte en route to the Greizer Hut (ZRR Stage 2)

state; it does not cover any aspect of medical repatriation. So even with an EHIC, you still need to be insured.

## THE AUSTRIAN ALPINE CLUB

Huts throughout the Zillertal are administered by the Austrian and German Alpine Clubs, the OeAV and DAV respectively, except for those in the South Tyrol that are owned and administered by the Italian Alpine Club (CAI) or its regional equivalent, the Alpenverein Sudtyrol (AVS)

The Oesterreichischer Alpenverein (OeAV), translated as the Austrian Alpine Association, was founded in 1862 to foster and encourage the sport of mountaineering and is largely credited to Franz Senn, who was the village priest in Neustift (Stubai valley)

until his untimely death, aged 52, from pneumonia, and his associates Johann Studl, a wealthy Prague business man, and Karl Hofmann, a young lawyer from Munich.

The Alpenverein, which celebrated its 150th anniversary in 2012, was the first alpine club to be established in mainland Europe. Presently the Club has just over 400,000 members in 195 *Sektions* that embrace all facets of mountaineering. Membership is open to any person who has a love of the mountains, regardless of age or ability.

The Club's principal activities include the development and provision of mountain huts, marking and maintenance of footpaths, production of maps, organising of mountaineering courses, and action on environmental issues, particularly those which are seen to spoil the mountains by either physical or visual pollution.

The establishment of the United Kingdom section, OeAV Sektion Britannia, is largely credited to Major Walter Ingham and Henry Crowther. It was formed in 1948 just after the Second World War to foster Anglo-Austrian relationships and to make it easier for British mountaineers in the immediate post-war years to visit the Eastern Alps.

Presently OeAV Sektion Britannia is one of the largest UK mountaineering clubs, with over 8000 members. The Club has a regular programme of indoor and outdoor meets, together with a website (see www.aacuk. org.uk) and quarterly newsletter.

The Club also runs training courses for its members, both in the UK and in Austria, through the Alpenverein Akademie mountaineering school. The Austrian Alpine Club (UK) enjoys full reciprocal rights agreements with all other alpine clubs in France (CAF), Switzerland (CAS), Italy (CAI) and Germany (DAV). This means that if you were to visit the South Tyrol in Italy to stay at the Schwarzenstein Hut, for example, you would pay the same fees as those enjoyed by members of the Italian Alpine Club and vice versa.

Anyone intending to undertake a hut-to-hut tour in Austria is strongly recommended to join OeAV Sektion Britannia (see Appendix B for full contact details).

*Above Schwarzsee, with Turnerkamp (left) and the Grosser Moseler (centre) (ZRR Stage 4)*

### MOUNTAIN HUTS

The word 'hut' is a misnomer. All the huts in the Zillertal as described here are more akin to mountain inns or guest houses that provide overnight accommodation and some form of restaurant service (see 'Meals and menus' below). This means that the mountain traveller does not need to return to the valley every few days to stock up on provisions.

There are well over 1000 huts in Austria, half of which are owned by the Austrian and German Alpine Clubs. In the Zillertal there are 30 OeAV and DAV huts, most of which are open from the end of June to mid-September. All the huts in the Zillertal have a resident guardian (Huettenwirt), who traditionally was a mountain guide (Bergfuehrer). Each hut has simple sleeping accommodation in the form of mixed dormitories (Matratzenlager) with blankets and pillows, and a small number of bedrooms (Bettzimmer) with duvets and sheets.

In addition to sleeping accommodation, each hut has some form of restaurant service offering a number of traditional dishes (see Appendix C for a glossary of menu terms). The menu generally comprises soup, a choice of main meals, Bergsteigeressen (literally 'mountain climbers' food'), cold meats, cheese and sometimes cakes and sweets. All huts serve drinks, tea, coffee, beer, wine and so forth, and most huts have a small shop where visitors can buy postcards, chocolate and biscuits.

On arrival at the hut, you should first remove your boots and store them in the boot rack, which will be close to the front door. You should also hang

*A smiling face awaits you at the end of your day's walk*

your ice axe, crampons, rope and other clobber on the racks provided, since such paraphernalia is not permitted in dormitories and bedrooms. If you are wet on arrival, your waterproofs should be shaken as dry as possible outside and hung up to dry with your ice tackle. If you are in a group, do not mill around the doorway, and again if you are wet make sure your group leaves outside as much water and dirt from boots as possible. Many of the huts are spotlessly clean, and for the benefit of all guests would like to remain that way.

You should then establish contact with the hut guardian to obtain your overnight accommodation. You will usually find this most important person in the kitchen (Kuche), dining room (Gaststube) or office (Bureau). A maximum of three nights is the Club rule, but this is not generally rigidly enforced. (Note that members have priority when accommodation is busy.)

Having found the guardian it is important to greet him or her ('Gruss Gott') and to explain that you would like some accommodation. The Huettenwirt is then likely to ask if you are Alpenverein and to ask for your membership card, which may be retained overnight or until such time as you leave, when you will be asked to pay.

If you do not speak German and feel uncomfortable asking for rooms in German, then write down and read out the following phrase 'Ich/ wir hatte gern ein zimmer oder matratzenlager, bitte' ('I/we would like a room, please'). Be polite by asking *bitte* when handing over the message and answering *danke* ('thank you') when the message is returned. Trivial as this may seem, these polite gestures are extremely important and will go a long way to ensuring a pleasant stay.

If the hut is full you may have to take residence in the Winterraum, which is usually the preserve of ski-mountaineers and those visiting when the hut is closed. The Winterraum is generally an annexe to the hut and may double as a storeroom or shelter for animals (as is the case at the Greizer Hut). Although the Winterraum can be quite cosy, remember to keep your gear off the floor out of reach of any mice.

Should the hut be beyond full, you will be provided with a mattress for Notlager, which roughly translated means 'sleeping with the furniture' – be it on the floor, in the corridors, on tables, on benches, or simply anywhere you can lie down. In the Zillertal this is a rare scenario, which results in some cosy, if somewhat noisy, situations.

Only on very rare occasions will you be asked to move on by the Huettenwirt, but only when bed space has been secured at an adjacent hut and only when there is sufficient daylight for you to reach your destination.

At the hut you will also require a sheet sleeping bag or Schlafsack for

At the Olperer Hut – it doesn't come much better than this!

use with the blankets and bedding which the hut provides. This is to minimise the amount of washing required and any water pollution downsteam of the hut. The sheet sleeping bag is a compulsory requirement, and if you do not have one the Huettenwirt will tell you to hire one.

You will also need to bring with you a pair of lightweight shoes or a pair of socks to wander around the hut, as boots upstairs are strictly forbidden (Verboten).

Each hut will have some form of male and female washrooms and toilet facilities, which vary from excellent at the Berliner and Olperer Huts to more modest at Friesenberg Haus and Greizer Huts. Elsewhere in the hut, usually near the front door, is the drying room (Trockenraum), where wet clothes can be dried.

The heart and soul of the hut is the dining room (Gaste Stube). Here you will find all manner of activities going on – from groups planning their next day, people celebrating a climb or a birthday, to people just chatting. It is a feeling best described by the German word 'Gemutlichkeit', which means 'homely' and 'friendly', and is something that is fostered and cherished throughout the whole of Austria.

At the end of your stay remember to make your bed and fold your blankets, to look around to make sure nothing is forgotten, and to search out the Huettenwirt and thank him and his staff for a pleasant stay. Remember to collect your membership card if it has not been given back to you. You should then fill in the hut book to record your stay and to indicate where you are going next.

## Hut information and reservations

As more and more huts in the Zillertal develop websites and are accessible by email, it is easier than ever to check for up-to-date hut information and make a reservation (see the Hut Directory, at the end of this guide, and Appendix B for contact details). For small groups of three or four people it is not necessary to make a reservation at the huts. However, groups of six plus are strongly advised to make contact with the hut before they go by post (sending a prepaid stamped addressed envelope for a reply), telephone, email or the hut website.

It is worth noting that members are allowed only three consecutive nights at any one hut, although this is not strictly enforced.

## Cancellations

Because huts can be booked over the internet and by telephone, abuse of this facility is beginning to become an issue. When reservations are made and people do not turn up, this results not just in a loss of business for the huts but also in a significant waste of food. Some huts are now asking for deposits to offset some of this risk. It is worth noting that in Austrian law

*At Friesenberg Haus (ZRR Stage 7)*

if you make a reservation and do not allow adequate time for a cancellation then you are still liable to pay the bill in full or in part. Remember that most huts are businesses, and it is only polite, if you have to cancel your reservation, to make every effort to contact the hut to inform them. If not, don't be surprised if you get billed.

## Meals and menus

All huts have some sort of restaurant service to cover the three daily meals, breakfast (Fruehstuck), lunch (Mittagessen) and dinner (Abendessen).

**Breakfast** is served from about 06.00 to about 07.30. Thereafter no meals are available until lunchtime as the hut staff are busy with general

house-keeping. Breakfast is the meal generally regarded as the worst value for money – but unless you are carrying your own provisions you will have little choice other than to accept it.

**Lunchtime** is usually from 12.00 to 14.00, but varies depending on the hut. However, it is possible to purchase simple meals like soup, Kase Brot and Apfelstrudl at most of the huts throughout the afternoon.

**Dinner** is the main meal of the day and is generally served from 18.00 to 19.30. In addition to meals listed on the menu, Bergsteigeressen will be available. Literally translated it means 'mountain climbers' food', and is a low-priced meal containing a minimum of 500 calories. The meal generally comprises spaghetti or pasta, potatoes, some meat or sausage, and sometimes a fried egg or a

dumpling. There is no hard-and-fast rule to this meal – other than it is relatively inexpensive and that there is usually a lot of it!

Breakfast usually comprises two or three slices of bread, a portion of butter, jam and cheese, with a choice of tea or coffee. If you do not finish it, take it with you – as you have paid for it all! Lunch and dinner are the main meals of the day and are served with a selection of vegetables or salad, and there will be vegetarian (Vegetarische) options. Drinks are served in quarter (Viertel) or half (Halbe) litres, or large (Gross) or small (Klein), and maybe hot (Heiss) or cold (Kalt). Tea, coffee, hot chocolate, lemonade, cola, beer, wine and schnapps are all available at the huts. See Appendix C, which lists many items found on a typical hut menu (Speisekarte), as well as some useful words and phrases for reading menus or ordering food and drink.

Generally the procedure for ordering meals is that you first organise a table. There is no formality, but sometimes when mountaineering training courses are being run, groups of tables may be marked 'private' (Privat) or 'reserved' (Reservierung). Having sat down, one of the waitresses (Fraulein) will take your order. Alternatively, you may have to go to the counter or kitchen (Kuche) to order, or there may be a sign saying 'Selbsbedienungs' ('self-service').

Because of the excellent service the huts provide very little of one's own food needs to be carried. However, many people do take with them their own basic rations – tea, coffee, bread, cheese, and so on. This allows them to make their own snacks and, by borrowing cups and purchasing *eine litre teewasser*, allows them to brew up for a small cost.

The only facility not provided at huts is for self-catering, and it does seem a little pointless when all the meals are reasonably priced.

The general rule is to pay an accumulative bill for food and drink. Visitors are therefore advised to make notes of their consumption to aid checking at the time of payment. Take note, these bills/lists can be considerable when staying at a hut for more than a couple of nights.

As a guideline for working out a budget, typical meal price lists can be obtained from the UK Section of the Austrian Alpine Club (www.aacuk. org.uk). At the time of writing, the cost of dinner in a hut was similar to prices in most British pubs for a decent bar meal plus drinks. Half board is currently €35–40, depending on the category of the hut.

## MAPS AND GUIDEBOOKS

### Maps
The following maps are required for both tours in this guide. The maps are published by the Austrian Alpine Club and available from the UK Section of the Austrian Alpine Club (www.aacuk. org.uk).

*On the Schwarzensteinkees glacier at the Schwarzensteinsattel (ZSTT Stage 7), with Grosser Moerchner to the right (note the knotted rope)*

**Alpenvereinskarte Zillertal Alpen**

Sheet 35/1    Westliches (West) scale 1:25,000
Sheet 35/2    Mittler (Central) scale 1:25,000

Also recommended, covering the complete region at a glance and available from major map retailers, are

- Freytag & Berndt Wanderkarte: Sheet 152, scale 1:50,000, *Mayrhofen, Zillertal Alpen, Gerlos-Krimml*
- Kompass Wanderkarte: Sheet 37, scale 1:50,000, *Zillertaler Alpen; Tuxer Alpen*

**Books**

For guidebooks and other reading see Appendix D.

**Websites**

These are currently in German but they will inevitably at some stage be translated into English.

- www.zillertal.at
- www.berlinerhoehenweg.at

## ALPINE WALKING SKILLS AND EQUIPMENT

How do the skills and equipment needed for walking in the Zillertal differ from those required for elsewhere?

## Boots

A relatively stiff boot with good ankle support and a stout vibram-type rubber sole is essential. Many of the walks involve sustained hard walking over rocky slopes and glacial debris, and encounters with patches of old hard snow. It is important to think of your boots as tools that can be used to kick steps and jam into rocky cracks without causing damage to your feet. While bendy boots may be a bit lighter and more comfortable, they are no match for a good pair of four-season mountaineering boots when it comes to dealing with difficult ground.

Construction of a rudimentary harness

## Instep crampons or microspikes

While crampons are normally associated with climbing, a pair of these little tools often comes in very handy when the weather decides to dump some unseasonable snow in July or August,

Alpine walking equipment

and they may just help provide that little extra security when you get up close to some old hard-packed snow.

## Improvised harness

Many of the routes are equipped with fixed wire ropes to provide some support over bits of difficult terrain. While these may be relatively easy to cross, the consequences of a fall should be borne in mind. In addition, not everyone is vertigo free, and the use of an improvised harness helps to provide confidence and security of passage. Constructed from a 2.4m long by 10mm wide Dyneema sling, three or four overhand knots, and a large jumbo-sized screw-gate karabiner, this harness (pictured) will allow you to clip into those fixed wires whenever the need arises and arrest a fall when you least expect it.

**Trekking poles**

Poles are almost standard accessories for most people these days, but in the Alps they come into their own – being very handy when crossing glacial steams and for traversing steep patches of old snow.

**Glacier travel**

The glaciers of the Zillertal are in the heartland of the Tyrol and the Eastern Alps. Quite a few of the mountaineering routes ('Excursions') described in this guide involve crossing or negotiating glaciers that can be crevassed depending on the time of year and vary from season to season. Indeed

*It's better to practise this on safe ground before you go, rather than having to 'practise' in a real-life situation*

the ascent of the Grosser Loeffler (ZRR Excursion 3.1) is classed as the most crevassed climb in the Zillertal.

Although crevasses (Spalten) will be encountered they should not create a serious problem for the mountain traveller and most will be easily bypassed. As is common to most glaciers, the main crevasse zone is on the steep sections, at the edges, and where the ice breaks away from the underlying rocks to form bergschrunds (Randkluft). If difficulties do arise it will be in negotiating bergschrunds such as those that exist below the Grosser Loeffler on the Floiten Kees glacier.

In the route description orientation on the glacier is described as being in the direction of flow along the right- or left-hand bank. This means that in ascent the left bank will be on your right. To avoid confusion, as may happen when route finding in mist, a compass bearing has been added in the route description to aid direction.

While most of the Zillertal's glaciers are relatively straightforward, they can vary quite considerably from season to season, the Floiten Kees and Schlegeis Kees glaciers being good examples. This scenario is further exacerbated by large temperature variations, generally because of the glaciers' relatively low altitude. This means that while routes may be straightforward one year, with minimal snowfall in the following year, previously hidden crevasses may become exposed and enlarged. The result is that glacier travel becomes more problematic.

The ideal number of people for glacier travel is four. Two is the absolute minimum, and solo travel should be avoided for obvious reasons. A party of two could gain some extra security by teaming up with a second party, gaining strength through weight of numbers.

Many of the Zillertal's glaciers are dry glaciers at their lower levels and are quite safe to traverse unroped, as the crevasses are obvious and easily avoided. However, when crevasses pose a threat – for example where they overlap, are deep, and occur on steep ground, as is found on the Grosser Loeffler – then the party should be roped up. Equally, parties should be roped at all times while crossing glaciers that are snow covered, such as those on the Schwarzenstein Kees glacier on the approach to the Berliner Hut, no matter how well trodden the route. It is worth remembering that crevasses have no respect for people and can open up beneath the best of us.

For a roped party of three, the group leader (the most experienced person) is best placed in the middle, since it is the group leader who will contribute most to a rescue in the event of a mishap. The second most experienced person should take the lead position at the head of the rope in order to route find and the last person, preferably the heaviest, should take a place at the back to act as the anchor.

For parties visiting the Alps for the first time, particularly those of equal ability, some experimenting will be necessary to gain more experience. However, it is absolutely essential that you practise roping up and crevasse rescue before you go, particularly a crevasse rescue scenario in which the fallen climber is out of sight of his companions and another member of the party has to go to their assistance and enter the crevasse, as would be the case if your companion were hurt.

## A tried and tested crevasse rescue technique

The following technique is suggested (only 'suggested' because the style varies between German- and French-speaking parts of the Alps). If you learned glacier and crevasse techniques in the Western Alps you may well have been taught a different but equally valid approach. This method works and will ensure that a group has a safe anchor at all times.

In ascent and descent the lightest person should go first at the front to route find. Should the route finder fall into a crevasse (unlikely) it is improbable that the rest of the group will be dragged in after them, but in a full-on fall you will be dragged off your feet. In case such a mishap occurs then the heaviest person is best placed at the back to act as anchor. For a party of two the most experienced person should be at the back in both ascent and descent.

To rope up a party of three, the middle man (group leader) should tie on 15m from one end of the rope, with the rope leader tied on at the front end. The back man (anchor) should then tie on about 12m behind the middle man (group leader). The surplus rope at the end should then be coiled by the anchorman and carried over the shoulder and rucksack or, as the author prefers, it can be loosely coiled inside the top of the rucksack, from where it can be easily retrieved in the event of being needed for a crevasse rescue. In addition to roping up, two Prusik loops are needed for attaching to the rope by each person, to be stored in their pockets.

On most glaciers the party will move together, keeping a respectable distance between each person. When there is no crevasse danger a few rope coils may be carried in the hand of each person to make the rope more manageable and to help prevent it snagging and being dragged along the glacier's surface, making the rope wet and heavy.

When crevasse zones are encountered, the rope between individuals should be kept taut to limit the effect of a fall. Where crevasses pose a very real risk, such as when they are large or their extent is unknown, the rope leader's second (middle man) should belay, while the rope leader traverses or jumps the crevasse. At the same time the group's anchorman will be similarly belayed a safe distance away. While these procedures may seem complicated and time-consuming, with a little practice they should become second nature.

The purpose behind these techniques is to prevent climbers falling into crevasses and to ensure glaciers are crossed safely. Most mountaineers will spend many hours crossing glaciers without any serious mishap. Experienced mountaineers will be able to recall falling into crevasses up to the waist, a few to the chest and the odd one falling through the surface to the glacier below. In most instances during a fall climbers can react quickly enough to spread their weight by outstretching their arms or by falling backwards to prevent themselves falling further. Once the fall is arrested, the group's second (the group leader) should belay while the anchorman uses their weight and position to secure the belay, which then frees the group leader to make use of the anchorman's coiled spare rope to effect the rescue and haul the leader free.

Should the leader fall free and end up inside the crevasse, it is important that the rest of the party work quickly. If the leader has fallen into a concealed crevasse it is likely that they will be hurt. This is due to the fact that their rucksack will have jarred, pushing the head forward and banging it on the ice during the fall. In such situations there are a number of options to choose from, but all will be useless unless the group has spent a little time practising crevasse rescue techniques. This is absolutely essential.

# Assisted Hoist Rope Pulley method of crevasse rescue

**A** short Prusik to secure the rope to the buried ice axe belay
**B** Prusik belay to secure the rescuer
**B1** moves up and down on the dead rope as needed
**C** Prusik bewteen the live and dead ropes
**C1** allows for the rope to be locked off between hauls. Allows rescuer the opportunity to rest and 'let go' of the rope
**C2** allows rescuer to move

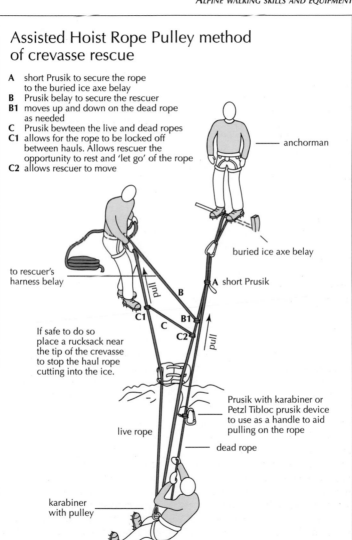

anchorman

buried ice axe belay

to rescuer's harness belay

**A** short Prusik

**B**

pull

**C1**

**B1**

**C**

**C2**

pull

If safe to do so place a rucksack near the tip of the crevasse to stop the haul rope cutting into the ice.

live rope

Prusik with karabiner or Petzl Tibloc prusik device to use as a handle to aid pulling on the rope

dead rope

karabiner with pulley

In this situation, provided the rope leader is uninjured, it may be possible to:
- simply haul them out of the crevasse using brute force
- help the rope leader to Prusik out of the crevasse under their own steam
- by lowering the end of the surplus rope, rescue the rope leader by using a combination of hauling and Prusiking using the Assisted Hoist Rope Pulley method (see diagram previous page).

If the rope leader is injured, then the actual group leader will have to go into the crevasse to perform first aid and secure the second haulage rope. Thereafter, once the group leader (the middle man if there are three of you) is back on the surface it is just about possible for the group leader and anchorman to haul the rope leader to the surface, using the Prusik loops to lock off the hauling rope. In this scenario a full-blown mountain rescue is perhaps the correct decision.

The UK Section of the Austrian Alpine Club organises basic training for glacier crossing and crevasse rescue through the OeAV Alpenverein Akademie. Contact the AAC (UK) Office for details, www.aacuk.org.uk.

The National Mountain Centre at Plas y Brenin also runs similar introductory courses. Contact www.pyb.co.uk.

A DVD of 'Alpine Essentials' is also available from the British Mountaineering Council (BMC), www.thebmc.co.uk.

## KIT LIST

A good general principle is: one on, one off and the odd spare. Also, if you are travelling as a group try to share equipment to minimise the weight each person has to carry. For example, you will only need one comprehensive first aid kit, one repair kit, one set of maps, one guidebook, one phrase book, one pair of binoculars and one set of spare batteries, if all the headlamps are the same.
- Rucksack (50 litre)
- Boots (suitable for all seasons)
- Trekking poles (optional)
- Long socks (2 pairs
- Short socks (3 pairs)
- Trousers or breeches
- Shorts (optional)
- Underwear (3 pairs)
- Shirts (2)
- Light fleece pullover
- Light windproof jacket
- Waterproofs, jacket and trousers
- Hat, gloves
- Gaiters (optional)
- Headlamp or torch
- Toiletries plus small towel
- Water bottle or thermos flask
- First aid kit with sun cream and lip salve
- Sunglasses plus spare
- Repair kit: needle and thread, super glue, candle, binding wire

*Be prepared for all sorts of terrain*

- Pocket knife
- Selection of polythene bags
- Maps and compass
- Whistle
- Notepad and pencil
- Zillertal guide book
- Emergency gear, bivvy bag, food rations
- Personal optional items, such as German phrase book, camera, binoculars

**Also recommended for walkers**
- one set of instep crampons or microspikes
- one 2.4m long x 10mm wide Dyneema tape sling
- Large screwgate karabiner

Should you intend to **climb some of the peaks** then you will need to add the following to the above list and know how to use them.
- Ice axe
- Crampons

- 2 large slings with screw gate karabiners
- 3 Prussik loops
- Climber's harness
- Ice screw
- 2 spare karabiners
- Length of climber's rope such as 50m x 9mm for each group of 3 people
- A small selection of slings with nuts, a pulley, universal rock piton and (for crevasse rescue) 5 karabiners

**Other items useful for a group**
- Altimeter
- Ice hammer
- Dead boy snow belay
- Figure of eight abseil device
- Prusiking devices such as Petzl, Tibloc or Wild Country Ropeman

**Hut wear**
- Lightweight change of clothes
- Hut shoes or socks
- Trousers

- Shirt
- Sheet sleeping bag
- Inflatable pillow

## USING THIS GUIDE

### Paths, tracks and waymarks

Paths throughout the Zillertal are waymarked roughly every hundred metres or so with a daub of red paint. At intersections, paths frequently have a signpost or alternatively have a red and white paint marker with a designated path number; this in turn is cross-referenced to maps and guidebooks, including this one.

Paths throughout both the routes in this guide vary from traditional mountain paths to tracks across boulder fields and rough ground. Walkers will also encounter steep ground, late summer snow and fixed wire ropes here and there that are installed to aid your stability. Paths for hut-to-hut routes are frequently marked with a signpost just outside the hut that gives the standard time in hours for the distance between huts without stops.

The tracks onto and across glaciers are not normally marked, as the route may vary from year to year. Anyone venturing onto glaciers is expected to have the necessary know-how and route-finding skills. However, sometimes local guides will place marker poles on the glacier to aid route finding, such as those on the heavily crevassed Floiten Kees glacier.

Note that in this guide, where the route follows a river, stream or glacier, any mention of the 'left' or 'right' bank refers to the 'true left' or 'true right', that is, when when looking downstream. This means that in ascent the left bank will be on your right. To avoid confusion, efforts have been made throughout the text to add a compass bearing to ensure walkers go in the right direction!

Given the above, no great demand will be made on the individual's route-finding skills when following the routes in the guide, except for the occasional issue noted in the text. However, as with all mountains, the Zillertal included, route finding is made much more difficult in mist, rain and snow.

See Appendix C for a glossary of German–English words, including mountain terminology, which may be useful when route finding and navigating in the Zillertal Alps.

### Route descriptions and sketch maps

The routes described in the guide follow recognised paths and tracks corresponding to those indicated on maps and signposts. However, to aid route finding across unfamiliar ground, each daily tour itinerary is fully described and illustrated with a sketch map indicating the main topographical features en route. While the information provided is as accurate as possible, this may change from year to year due to landslips, avalanches and

*Some typical signs and waymarks – 'Bleib am Weg!' means 'Keep to the path!'*

*Hochfeiler (3510m) summit view along the frontier ridge and north face*

*At the Untere Weisszint Scharte looking towards the Stubai Alps (ZSTT Stage 4), Hochfeiler hut circled*

erosion (see www.cicerone.co.uk for any updates).

### Route grading

The routes described are suitable for people who are already involved in some sort of mountain activity on a regular basis. The tours are moderately, and sometimes quite, strenuous and require the ability to carry a full rucksack for over 6 hours a day. In terms of alpine grading, the majority of both routes falls into the mountaineering grade of easy to moderate. They comprise sustained mountain walking that requires the ability to negotiate steep ground, scramble over rocks, cross late summer snow and make use of fixed wire ropes; and a good head for heights is needed.

The ascents of the peaks are all graded mountaineering routes. They range from easy (as in the alpine grade 'Facile' or simply F) with no significant difficulties, such as the ascent of the Hoeher Riffler (ZRR Stage 7), to those peaks that are moderately difficult to climb and need mountaineering skills (having the alpine grade 'Peu Difficile' or PD), such as the ascent of the Grosser Moseler (ZRR Stage 5) and Olperer (ZRR Stage 6), which have a number of short but not sustained difficulties.

### Standard times

At the beginning of each route description a 'standard time' in hours (Stunden) is given as an estimate of time required from hut to hut. This standard time is generally on the generous side compared to that given in the Alpenvereins 'Hut Directory', also known as the 'Green Hut Book'. The standard time stated is for the hours spent moving and does not include lunch stops and other breaks. Most British parties find some difficulty in meeting quoted standard times, particularly in the early days of a trek. Be advised that this is of no consequence, as a good number of standard times are unattainable and seem to have been set by Olympic athletes. With this in mind, the route descriptions in this guide give the actual time required when carrying a more than full heavy touring rucksack. The times are walking times only and do not include breaks, long lunches or the like.

Walkers undertaking the ZRR with children are advised to add at least 1hr to the standard time to allow for frequent picnic stops. Similarly, aspirant alpinists should make due adjustment to the standard time while they learn the rudiments of glacier travel and the very time-consuming activity of roping up and getting crampons on and off.

**Note** The timings given for ascents from the huts (detailed separately at the end of several stage descriptions) are the outward time only (one way). The round trip may take up to twice as long.

### Spellings

You may well encounter discrepancies in the spelling of place names between those used in this guide and those found on signposts, in the huts and on maps. This is an issue across German-speaking countries that use the *eszett* letter (for 'ss') and umlauts on 'o' and 'u'. In practice this shouldn't cause confusion as long as travellers are aware of it. In this guidebook the *eszett* is presented as a double 's' (as in *weiss*), and umlauts are replaced by o/oe, u/ue, as appropriate.

### Professional mountain guides

Professional mountain guides (Bergfuehrer) can be hired if you so wish. See Appendix B for more information.

# ZILLERTAL RUCKSACK ROUTE (HOEHENWEG)

*Crossing the Gamsleiten en route to the Gams Hut, with Hochfeiler in the distance (ZRR Stage 8)*

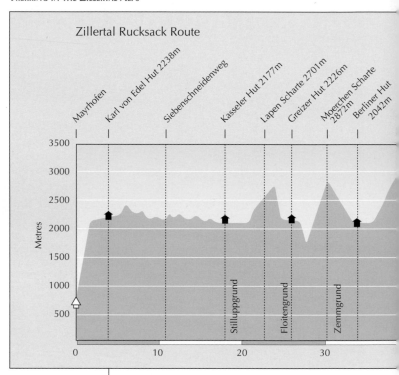

A good place to start might be to clarify the Rucksack Route's various names and outline the stages of development that it has been through over many years before becoming the fine tour we know today.

This guidebook uses the 'Zillertal Rucksack Route', the name given to the tour in English immediately after the Second World War as a simple description of what was needed to undertake the route – nothing more than a rucksack and pair of boots. This was around the same period that the UK section of the Austrian Alpine Club (OeAV Sektion Britannia) was born (1948), and until this time the Berliner Zillertal Hoehenweg (its German name) was unknown in the English-speaking world.

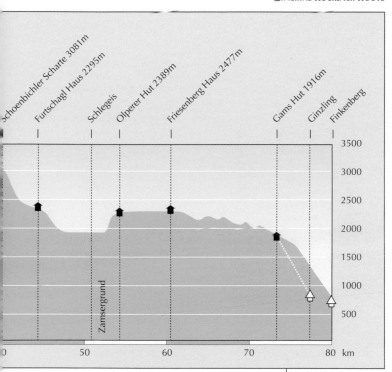

The tour is known as the Berliner Hoehenweg (Berliner High Level Way) in Germany and as the Zillertaler Runde Tour (Zillertal Round Tour) in Austria. The former name has arisen because the DAV German Alpine Club Sektion Berlin owns the majority of the huts (in fact, all the huts are in ownership of various Sektions that make up the Deutscher Alpenverein).

The original route of the early 1900s comprised only the Greizer, Berliner and Furtschagl Haus hut connections, when access from Mayrhofen up the valley of the Dornaubergtal to Ginzling and Breitlahner was very limited. Indeed access beyond the huts to the remote valleys of Floitental-Gunggl (Greizer), Zemmgrund (Berliner) and

51

Zamsergrund (Furtschagl Haus) was almost non-existent, making such journeys expeditions in their own right. The Kasseler to Greizer Hut connection was added around 1930, again with limited access via the Stillupptal valley.

The route then remained virtually unchanged for the next 30 years. The Karl von Edel to Kasseler Hut connection was added during the early 1970s due to the deployment of their excellent pioneering and route-finding skills over many years by the DAV members from Sektions Wurzburg and Aschaffenberg.

The route's main development era was a spin-off of the hydro-electricity project of the late 1960s and early 1970s, when the building of construction service roads led to improved access up all the side-valleys. In particular, the road built beyond Breitlahner to Schlegeis opened up access considerably to Furtschagl Haus and made possible the link in 1976 between Furtschagl Haus and the Olperer Hut, with the Friesenberg Haus being included as a natural addition. The Gams Hut connection was added to the tour around 1977, when hunting paths around the various high alms (groups of farm buildings) were linked together and those that were overgrown were cleared of vegetation.

The route today starts at Mayrhofen and goes first to the Karl von Edel Hut, then to the Kasseler, Greizer, Berliner, Furtschagl, Olperer, Friesenberg and Gams Huts before returning to Mayrhofen.

The length of the tour is 70–80km, depending on where you start and finish, and it ascends some 6700m. The route can be undertaken in any direction, although the clockwise course (as described here) is seen as moderately easier and is the preferred direction also because of the proximity of the Edel Hut to Mayrhofen. In addition to the main route, this guide also includes a number of walking and climbing excursions to various peaks that can be undertaken from huts along the way.

As can be seen from the route summary table (see Appendix A) the demands of this tour will determine your confidence to do the full round. While the start and finish sections of the route are long in distance and duration, they are not overly demanding. Providing you plan for this and the weather is good, you should be fine. If you have children with you, you will need to err on the side of caution. It might be advisable for a family group to start at the Kasseler Hut (start of Stage 3) and end at the Friesenberg Haus (end of Stage 7).

An ascent of the Ahorn Spitze can also be undertaken as a day trip from Mayrhofen (see Stage 1).

*Gruss Gott und sehr gut Zillertal Bergtouren.*

# STAGE 1
### *Mayrhofen to the Karl von Edel Hut*

| | |
|---|---|
| **Start** | Mayrhofen (633m) |
| **Finish** | Karl von Edel Hut (2238m) |
| **Distance** | 3km |
| **Ascent** | 283m |
| **Standard time** | 3hrs |

A pleasant introduction to the Zillertal Rucksack Route. There is also time to climb the nearby Ahorn Spitze in the same day.

From the combined Zillertalbahn railway station and bus terminus cross the main road and turn right, heading south up the main road into **Mayrhofen**. After approximately 200m turn left before a garage-cum-filling station, following the road to the town centre, passing on the right-hand side first the very grand Elisabeth Hotel, then, a little further on, Mayrhofen's main post office.

On Mayrhofen's main street is the Alpine School and Mountain Guides Office owned by legendary Austrian mountaineer **Peter Habeler**. With Reinhold Messner from the South Tyrol he took the mountaineering world by storm with many audacious ascents, including the first oxygen-free ascent of Mount Everest. Their skill was summed up in their 10hr ascent of the North Face of the Eiger – even the most competent of climbers would take at least one full day. Habeler's companion went on to do greater things, eventually becoming the first person to climb all 14 peaks over 8000m.

From the post office, turn right at the road junction and continue the urban walk uphill for around 15mins, passing lots of shops and expensive-looking places until you reach the Penkenbahn cable-car station on the right-hand side. Pass this and continue to a bridge across the river. Turn left just after the bridge and follow the sign-posts for the **Ahornbahn/Filzenboden cable car**, which is reached after a further 5mins. Remember when purchasing your ticket the all-important 'Gruss Gott' ('God be with you') and ask for a one-way ticket (*einfach bitte*). Show your OeAV membership card to obtain a modest discount.

## Mayrhofen to the Karl von Edel Hut and ascent of the Ahorn Spitze

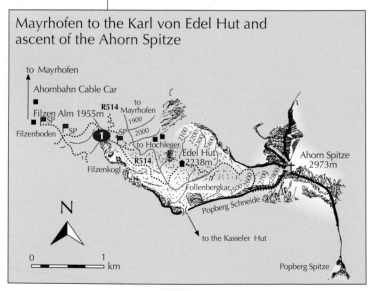

The cable-car ride takes around 5mins and provides excellent views across Mayrhofen as you are whisked high above the Zillertal valley in a cable car that boasts of being the largest in the Tyrol and is akin to a double-decker bus laid flat on its side.

From the upper cable-car station and restaurant at **Filzen Alm** (1955m), proceed onto the grassy terrace and follow signs for Route 514 and the Edel Hut.

The route follows a well-marked path east then southeast around the jagged ridge of the Filzenschneide into a rock garden with boulders of house-sized proportions, from where the hut at the base of the Ahorn Spitze west ridge is clearly visible. Follow the trail, which in summer is a very popular day's outing from Mayrhofen and a much frequented route to the **Edel Hut** (1½–2hrs).

*The Edel Hut and Ahorn Spitze as seen from the rock garden*

# EXCURSION 1.1
## Ascent of the Ahorn Spitze (2973m)

| | |
|---|---|
| **Start** | Edel Hut |
| **Distance** | 1.5km |
| **Ascent** | 735m |
| **Standard ascent time** | 2hrs |

The problem for the Edel Hut is that it is unfortunately very much a one-mountain hut, unless you are a day-tripper from Mayrhofen or en route to the Kasseler Hut. That aside, the Ahorn Spitze is a fine mountain in its own right that offers something of a challenge on its upper slopes and has some of the finest panoramic views in the region. Having dumped much of your gear at the hut, a very lightweight ascent can be made as an afternoon excursion through the mountain's west flank via the Follenbergkar, which roughly translated means 'rocks and boulders having fallen off the mountain'.

Be careful hereabouts as the ridge is very exposed.

The route starts off by following an old well-marked trail east along a glacial moraine, with signs 'Weg am Blieb' along the way telling would-be climbers to keep to the path. After about ¾hr a 'Gesperrt' sign is reached, which blocks off the old path that was obliterated by a rock avalanche in 2002 and directs you south across the stone-strewn couloir to a small but obvious col on the **Popberg Schneide** ridge (1hr). There are good views overlooking the Stilluppgrund valley towards the Kasseler Hut. ◄

From here, follow the obvious rocky ridge east, with occasional good scrambling (very exposed in places and needing a good head for heights), until after a short hour the ridge steepens considerably just below the rocks that form the true summit of the **Ahorn Spitze**. The lower second summit is visible just 100m away, so descend the rocks into a gap then scramble up once more to the large summit cross (about 2½hrs from the hut).

From the summit excellent views abound in all directions, especially to the south towards Mayrhofen and the long Zillertal valley. Elsewhere the big snow-capped peaks are just a little too far away to provide any serious interest, apart from the Grosser Loeffler to the south. However, the Gross Venediger, fourth highest peak in Austria, is obvious to the east, then closer at hand Brandberg Kolm to the northeast. Turning more east, the Zillergrund reservoir is visible, and finally, those with sharp eyes (perhaps assisted with binoculars) will be able to locate the Plauener Hut and Reichen Spitze.

From the summit the descent route is the same as the ascent, although a little more care is required to scramble down the steep rocks. Once at the little col take time to investigate the route to the Kasseler Hut (Stage 2), as the first part of the route along the Siebenschneidenweg around the Popbergkar couloir and boulder field is clear and obvious.

*'Gesperrt' sign advising that the way ahead (the original route) is closed*

The final scramble to the summit

# STAGE 2
## Karl von Edel Hut to the Kasseler Hut

| | |
|---|---|
| **Start** | Karl von Edel Hut (2238m) |
| **Finish** | Kasseler Hut (2177m) |
| **Distance** | 14km |
| **Ascent** | A lot of ups (720m) and similar downs (780m) |
| **Standard time** | 8–10hrs |
| **Notes** | The standard time is made up of 8½hrs for the journey, plus 1hr for stops and ½hr for any mishaps. This means you need to be on your way no later than 06.00. Arrange with the Huettenwirt to leave breakfast and thermos flasks on the dining room tables for an early start. |
| **Warning** | Crossing the many boulder fields and negotiating fixed ropes and steep grassy slopes absorbs time and saps concentration. This stage should be undertaken only in settled weather. There are few places to shelter and route finding in poor weather is not always straightforward. |

Despite the 'Nur Fuer Geubte' ('only for the experienced') warning sign outside the Edel Hut, which probably puts off a number of very capable groups, this is a very good long-distance walk and a fitting way to start the Rucksack Route that will satisfy most enthusiasts. The length of the walk is a good measure of personal fitness. The route traverses high above the steeply sided valley of Stilluppgrund, roughly on the 2300m contour line, and provides challenging terrain and excellent scenery throughout its length.

Once past the little col of Popbergneider, just beyond the Edel Hut, your attention will be firmly fixed to the south towards the splendid Grosser Loeffler (3379m) and across the valley to the sharp pointed peak of Gigalitz, as well as to the obvious col that is the Lapen Scharte.

First established during the 1970s by members of the DAV Wurzburg and Aschaffenburger Sektions, and not surprisingly named the Aschaffenburger Hohensteig, the route is now more popularly known as the **Siebenschneidenweg** ('seven ridges way'). There are indeed seven cols and spurs to be crossed on this excursion, as the name suggests.

From the **Karl von Edel Hut**, follow Route 519 (signposted) on a good path heading south, climbing first gradually then more steeply across rocky slopes. There are fixed ropes at the top leading to the little col (visible from the hut) called the **Popbergneider** (2448m, ¾hr), with its attendant little peak of **Popbergeggl**. ◀

*Excellent views and scenery as the route starts to open up.*

From the col, descend very steep rocks and grassy slopes, carefully aided by fixed wire ropes, and head east towards the large open combe of the **Popbergkar**. Cross this in a wide arc, first east then south through boulder fields to the foot of a rock face. A short and difficult scramble aided by fixed ropes follows to gain the ridge just to the east of the **Krummschnabel Scharte** col (2440m) on the southwest ridge coming down from the **Popberg Spitze** (2891m, 1¾hrs).

Cross the col, descend steep rocks diagonally across the rock face aided by fixed ropes, and again head first east then south across difficult open ground of large boulders and blocks across the **Hasenkar** couloir until stopped by the near vertical rock wall below the col of the **Sammerschartl** (2392m). Climb slowly up the 100m of very steep rocky slabs, aided by gymnasium-style ropes, to gain the col and **Nofertenschneide** ridge, on the southwest ridge of the Wilhelmer (2937m, 4hrs).

From the col, descend steep rocks, aided by fixed ropes, and cross the less demanding **Nofertenkar** boulder field to the **Nofertensmauer** rock wall on the Hennsteigenkam ridge (2277m, 1hr).

### Escape route
Should you be forced to consider abandoning the route you should do so at this point, as it is the only place on

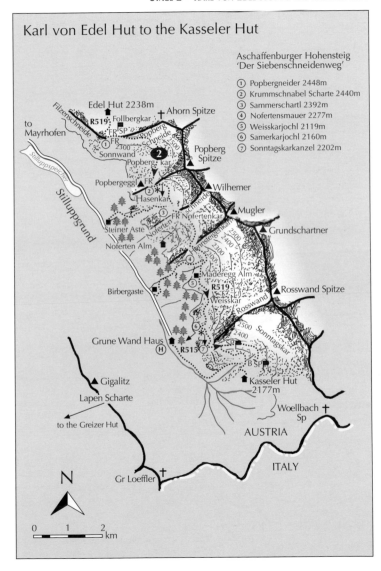

# Karl von Edel Hut to the Kasseler Hut

Aschaffenburger Hohensteig
'Der Siebenschneidenweg'

① Popbergneider 2448m
② Krummschnabel Scharte 2440m
③ Sammerschartl 2392m
④ Nofertensmauer 2277m
⑤ Weisskarjochl 2119m
⑥ Samerkarjochl 2160m
⑦ Sonntagskarkanzel 2202m

to Mayrhofen

Filzenschneide

Edel Hut 2238m
R519
FR SP
FR
① 2300
Sonnwand
Popberg kar
Popbergeggl
FR
②
*
Hasenkar

Ahorn Spitze
Popberg Schneide
Popberg Spitze
Wilhemer
Mugler

Stilluppspeicher

Stilluppgrund

Popbergneider

Popberg

Schneide

③ FR Nofertenkar

Steiner Aste
Noferten Alm

Grundschartner

Noferten

Schneide

2500
2400
2300

④

Maderegg Alm
R519
Weisskar

Birbergaste

⑤

Rosswand Spitze
Rosswand

Grune Wand Haus
(H)

⑥
*
⑦
R515

Sonntagskar
SP
2500
2400
B SP

Kasseler Hut
2177m

Gigalitz

Lapen Scharte

to the Greizer Hut

Woellbach
Sp

AUSTRIA

ITALY

N

Gr Loeffler

0    1    2
km

*At the Popbergneider
and Popbergeggl
peak*

the route that will allow a descent, descending east on
the north side of the col to pick up forest trails at Noferten
Alm, following the exceedingly steep tracks to the alm at
Stillupphaus. However, it is safer and easier to return to
the sanctuary of the Edel Hut despite having to reverse
the Sammerschartl, where a comfortable bed and good
food would make the return journey more acceptable.
Nevertheless, you should take into consideration that the

most difficult sections are behind you, that the terrain gets progressively easier, and that you are now just a little over halfway into completing the journey.

Continue south over broken ground, sometimes boulders, and then easy paths to make good time across the **Maderegg Alm**, where there are some semi-abandoned farm buildings. One of these huts has been patched up in recent years and is now equipped with a few beds to act as a bivi and sanctuary for the exhausted and as an emergency shelter from the weather – a good place to take a break. Thereafter, move across the **Weisskarjochl** to the **Samerkarjochl** col (2160m), on the southwest ridge of the Rosswand (1¾hr).

Cross the Samerkarl and Steinkarl combes on good paths to reach the last of the ridges to be crossed, the **Sonntagskarkanzel** (2202m). From this point you can see the Kasseler Hut, which looks tantalisingly close, and the track across the Lapen Scharte, on the route to the Greizer Hut, across the great void to the southwest.

From the col proceed east in a contouring traverse, descending steep grassy slopes interspersed with streams, then head south, losing a couple of hundred metres of height in the process, to a makeshift bridge (usually a single wooden plank) over fast-flowing streams and the junction with the path coming up the valley from Grune Wand Haus (signpost). Thereafter, follow the zigzag rocky path for a further ½hr to the **Kasseler Hut** (2hrs).

## TAKING CHILDREN

If you have young people with you, you need to be absolutely sure that they can complete the journey without risk to themselves and without compromising the group's safety. To this end, they should not be overburdened with a heavy rucksack when loads can be shared among adults.

However, not to be too pessimistic, the author's daughter completed this walk when aged 14, carrying her own gear, including ice axe and crampons. More recently a 12-year-old was seen undertaking the route with his 65-year-old grandfather!

# EXCURSION 2.1

*Ascent of the Woellbach Spitze (3209m)*

| | |
|---|---|
| **Start** | Kasseler Hut |
| **Distance** | About 4km |
| **Ascent** | 1030m |
| **Grade** | F+ |
| **Standard ascent time** | 4hrs |

This is a justifiable and popular day's outing from the Kasseler Hut on a much underated peak. It involves a straightforward glacier climb, followed by a rock and snow ridge, with a scramble to finish. Because of its popularity, the normal route up the mountain is often a well-beaten trail. The route described here takes a slightly different approach by traversing the mountain from the Woellbachjoch col, and there is only a slight increase in difficulty by climbing it this way – via the southwest ridge.

The scenic interest up the mountain is excellent, with most of the approach being dominated by the mountain itself, while further on there are superb views across the void to the northeast face of the Grosser Loeffler. The panoramic view from the summit is extensive, particularly along the frontier ridge towards the Zillertal's central massif and east towards the Venediger group of mountains.

From the **Kasseler Hut** follow signpost directions for Route 502 to the first signpost and **junction** with the path to the Greizer Hut (15mins). Turn off left and continue uphill, zigzagging steeply through boulder fields, where after a further 10mins a signpost is reached indicating the way to the panoramic viewpoint of **Schone Aussicht**. Continue heading southwest over rocks and slabs until a large stone cairn is reached by the side of a **glacial pond-tarn** (1hr). Continue as before, threading a way over difficult ground of boulders and rickety blocks and heading southwest in the direction of an obvious rock buttress, noted as point **2532m** on the AV map at the foot of the remnants of the **Ostliches Stillupkees glacier** (1½hrs).

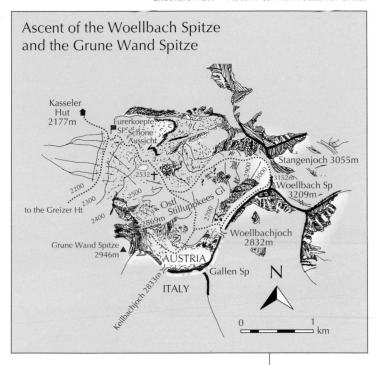

## Ascent of the Woellbach Spitze and the Grune Wand Spitze

Kasseler Hut 2177m

Eurerkoepfe SP Schöne Aussicht

to the Greizer Ht

2200
2300
2400
2500
2532
2869m

Ostl Stilluppkees Gl

Grune Wand Spitze 2946m

AUSTRIA

Keilbachjoch 2831m

ITALY

Gallen Sp

2700
2900
3000
3152m

Stangenjoch 3055m

Woellbach Sp 3209m

Woellbachjoch 2832m

N

0          1
└─────────┘ km

To traverse the mountain the route now crosses remnants of the glacier southwest, heading for the rocks and ridge below the **Woellbachjoch** col at 2832m. Cross the glacier, that while dormant still has some crevasse (*spalten*) interest and danger midway, then scramble up steep rocks, sometimes on the scrappy side, in a rising traverse right to left to reach the **col** at 2832m (2½hrs).

From the col, continue up the obvious ridge northeast, scrambling to and fro over difficult ground with loose boulders, blocks and patches of snow, as the route rises and cranks up a few degrees near the summit and onto the top with its large wooden cross at 3209m (4hrs). ▶

From the summit descend north by continuing to follow the natural line of the ridge. Descend steeply across

Excellent views into the Italian South Tyrol and to close neighbour the Grosser Loeffler.

*Ascent of the Woellbach Spitze*

Should you have time on your hands, at its base the glacier has a number of good and reasonably safe crevasses that can be used to practise crevasse rescue techniques.

difficult ground over and around large boulders, with fixed ropes in place, until the slope gradually eases to join the ridge at 3152m. Continue down the ridge, north, usually a snow slope, to the **Stagenjoch col** at 3055m (1hr).

Should the snow and the weather be good, walkers can make good time by bypassing the Stangenjoch – do this by making a more direct descent northwest onto the **Ostliches Stillupkees glacier** and heading for a rock island (*rognon*) in the centre of the glacier, avoiding the obvious crevasse danger en route.

From the rock island, continue down the glacier's right bank, north, heading for the point at **2532m** and with it familiar ground back to the **hut** (3hrs). ◄

The Woellbach Spitze is the first major snow peak to be encountered on the Rucksack Route, and care must be taken when negotiating the crevasses on the approach to the Woellbachjoch col and when descending to the Stagenjoch pass. The main difficulties, however, are in climbing the dubious rocks and boulders to first gain the Woellbachjoch col, followed by the very mixed ground of the southwest ridge to the summit.

# EXCURSION 2.2

*Ascent of Grune Wand Spitze (2946m)*

| | |
|---|---|
| **Start** | Kasseler Hut |
| **Distance** | 3km |
| **Ascent** | 768m |
| **Grade** | F |
| **Standard ascent time** | 3hrs |

This is an excellent excursion, with some stunning scenery on a peak that does not get the attention it deserves. Once on the ridge the mountaineering situation is superb, with lots of good alpine scenery – particularly views of the Grosser Loeffler and close neighbour the Woellbach Spitze. From the summit the views across the Italian South Tyrol of the Ahrntal valley and peaks of the Dolomites are superb.

From the **Kasseler Hut**, follow the route description for climbing the Woellbach Spitze (see above) as far as the **glacial pond** and large stone cairn and col on the 2500m contour (1hr).

Continue to head southeast into the boulder-strewn glacial corrie-type basin, crossing open, difficult ground for around 400m – look for cairns as the route is not well marked – before turning more south, heading for the foot of the east spur coming down from the summit. With the corrie headwall of the frontier ridge ahead, round the foot of the spur, keeping to the easier ground, and climb the gradually steepening slope until immediately below the **Keilbachjoch**.

From here to the northwest you will be able to see a small col on the ridge noted as point 2869m on the AV map. Make a rising diagonal traverse left to right (south to north) over difficult rocky ground of boulders to the col and junction with the mountain's north ridge (1hr). ▶

Excellent views from here of the Woellbach Spitze and Grosser Loeffler.

From this point on the route is obvious – scramble south along the ridge, ascending the crest over blocks and boulders and the dubious rocks to the **Grune Wand Spitze** (2946m, just under 1hr).

As the route is not well frequented, waymarkings (particularly in the middle part of the route) are all but none existent, and this makes route finding somewhat haphazard. The warden at the Kasseler Hut is keen to promote the Grune Wand Spitze as a mountain in its own right, and if the DAV Sektion Kassel get the funding to create a Klettersteige protected climbing route on the mountain, the normal route will get more traffic and become more apparent. The other main difficulty is that much of the route crosses difficult rocky ground of slabs and blocks that require quite a bit of care, particularly along the crest of the ridge.

# STAGE 3
*Kasseler Hut to the Greizer Hut*

| | |
|---|---|
| **Start** | Kasseler Hut (2177m) |
| **Finish** | Greizer Hut (2226m) |
| **Distance** | 7.5km |
| **Ascent** | 700m |
| **Standard time** | 6–7hrs |
| **Note** | 7hrs is a far more realistic time, more so if you have a heavy rucksack. |
| **Warning** | The main dangers are crossing the rock avalanche debris 1hr after leaving the hut, then patches of steep snow and the fixed rope section crossing the near vertical steep-sided Lapen Kar-Elsenklamm buttress. Remember these ropes are mainly for ski tourers who cross this area when the slopes are still covered with snow in the springtime. Anyone not vertigo free should stay close to a companion for moral support and assistance. |

This is a pleasant day's outing with no major obstacles. The track is well defined throughout, although perhaps made a little awkward in various places by patches of snow, rock avalanche debris and huge boulders. After the previous day's outing from the Karl von Edel Hut, many walkers would consider this to be a rest day of sorts!

The scenic interest is dominated early in the day by the view towards the Grosser Loeffler, and later by the view down the valley into Stilluppgrund and across the steep slopes that make up the Siebenschneidenweg – allowing almost the entire route to be seen from the Karl von Edel Hut to the Kasseler Hut.

Once over the Lapen Scharte new scenery is explored, with the extensive Floitenkees and Schwarzenstein glaciers, together with the Grosser Moseler and Zsigmondy Spitze, famed as a rock climbing peak. But the best scenery of the day is saved for the end, when the Greizer Hut comes splendidly into view, with spectacular wall-to-wall mountain scenery.

From the **Kasseler Hut** follow signposts for Route 502, marked as the 'Berliner Hoehenweg', initially going southeast to the junction with the track leading to the Woellbach Spitze (15mins) (signpost). Continue as before on the main track, turning now more southwest, and after a further 20mins come to a door in the middle of nowhere. ▶

'The door' is the work of German artist Gunther Rauch and is one of several doors he has erected in the Alps.

Immediately after the door cross a suspension bridge over the raging glacial meltwaters coming down from high above. A short distance further on, the well-defined track disappears altogether thanks to a rock avalanche that tore the track apart. Cross this area with care as the slope is unstable, and then continue as before, traversing the slopes in a wide arc roughly on the 2300m contour through extensive boulder fields of the **Eiskar** to a point approximately north of the Francbach Jochl on the Austrian–Italian border (1hr). ▶

Excellent scenery hereabouts.

The route now turns more or less north to traverse the steep slopes of the **Loefflerkar**. This mid-section is frequently dotted with patches of snow and meltwater streaming down from the upper slopes of the Loefflerkees glacier. Fixed ropes are provided to aid stability on the

# Kasseler Hut to the Greizer Hut and ascent of the Grosser Loeffler

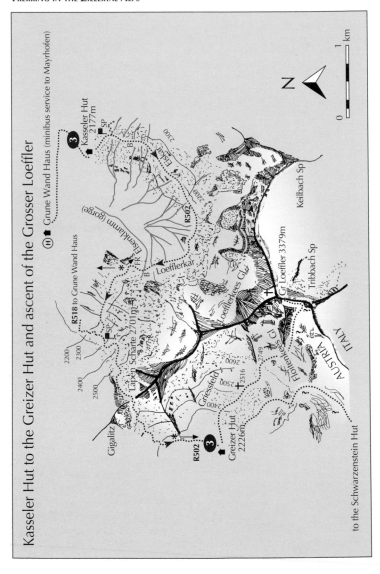

(H) Grune Wand Haus (minibus service to Mayrhofen)

way round the near vertical buttress and difficult sections that form the **Elsenklamm gorge** (3hrs). ▸

Great views back towards the Woellbach Spitze.

Continue northwest through the Lapenkar boulder field to join up with **Route 518** (signpost) on the 2800m contour marking the route coming up from Grune Wand Haus at the top end of the Stilluppgrund valley, located to the northeast (40mins).

The route turns southwest and continues to climb steeply in a series of long looping zigzags negotiating difficult ground through boulders of car-sized proportions and across patches of snow to the **Lapen Scharte** col (2701m), formed in a tight gap between the peaks of Gigalitz (3001m) and the slightly higher Greizer Spitze (3010m) (1½hrs; total time about 5hrs).

At the col there is excellent scenery, particularly across the void towards the Roswand Spitze in the east, with an opportunity to review the long walk from the Karl von Edel Hut – especially for those that made the effort to cross the Siebenschneidenweg! In the opposite direction

*Crossing the Loefflerkar boulder field, with Grosser Loeffler in the background*

*Descending from the Lapen Scharte (2701m), with the Moerchen Scharte on the horizon opposite, as seen en route to the Greizer Hut*

*'The door' – by artist Gunther Rauch*

there is time to scan the route to the Berliner Hut (Stage 4) across the Moerchen Scharte and ladder section at the foot of the ridge.

From the col, descend steeply southwest over rough broken ground through more boulder fields that have become a characteristic of this walk. At point 2400m, about 20mins from the Lapen Scharte, the route turns south into the **Griessfeld**, from where, after a short distance, the wonderfully sited **Greizer Hut**, complete with attendant peaks and gleaming glaciers, comes into superb view. The route, now obvious, continues along a fine paved rock gallery to the hut (1½hrs).

# EXCURSION 3.1

*Ascent of the Grosser Loeffler*

| | |
|---|---|
| **Start** | Greizer Hut |
| **Distance** | 4km |
| **Ascent** | 1153m |
| **Grade** | PD+ |
| **Standard ascent time** | 5hrs |
| **Note** | The route carries an alpine grade of Peu Difficile Plus (with sustained but moderate difficulties) and requires good mountaineering skills. |

The Grosser Loeffler is one of the best and most interesting mountains in the Zillertal. The route is mostly a glacier tour, with a demanding and teasing exercise in route finding on the Floitenkees glacier that deservedly gives the route the title of the most crevassed climb in the Zillertal!

The scenic interest is excellent throughout and in particular the glacial scenery is superb, not only in the immediate vicinity of the Floitenkees glacier but also across the great expanse of ice across to the Schwarzenstein. One cannot help wondering how much longer such an expanse of ice can last as the environment adjusts to global warming.

While the route prior to getting on the glacier is straightforward apart from negotiating ankle-twisting, leg-snapping jumbo-sized boulders, you are advised to do a route-finding venture before leaving the hut, as the trail is not well marked. Once on the glacier, good judgement will be required to navigate a route through the labyrinth of crevasses, some of which are in complex groups, and this complexity will have to be reversed in descent. If you are not entirely sure of your route-finding skills, consider building small stone cairns every 50m to aid your return.

From the **Greizer Hut**, the route starts off immediately uphill, heading southeast over rocks through the **Greissfeld** boulder field, making for point **2516m** on the AV map (1hr).

*The route as seen from the Tribbachsattel (on Stage 4)*

Continue southeast over difficult ground through rocks of car-sized proportions and other general glacial debris, often with patches of snow, to a point below the Kleiner Loeffler (2749m), where it should be possible (depending on seasonal conditions) to get onto the **Floitenkees glacier**'s north right bank (1hr).

Tackle up and get onto the glacier and proceed first south to round a buttress and the foot of a ridge. Then turn southwest heading up the glacier, negotiating several crevasse zones in parallel and lateral groups, some of which are quite complex and demand care. Once past the foot of the Loeffler's west ridge proper, proceed east up the steep glaciated slope bypassing crevasses en route and heading for point 3292m on the ridge between the Grosser Loeffler and the Tribbach Spitze. At a point below the ridge with its attendant Bergschrund, make a rising traverse north, keeping left to gain the upper slopes of the west ridge where it abuts the main south ridge (1½hrs).

It is hereabouts that a **light aircraft** crashed in 1996 sadly killing its occupants. While there may still be odd bits of the aircraft on the mountain, most of the wreckage has been removed by the Austrian military.

Get onto the rocks and climb the very steep difficult mixed ground over rocks and snow to gain the south ridge proper, followed by a short distance to **Grosser Loeffler**'s summit (3379m) with its large metal cross (1½hrs). ▶ Excellent mountaineering.

The first ascent of the mountain was made by Martin Lipolt and party in 1850.

The panoramic views from the summit are extensive in all directions. To the north are the mountains of the Karwendal on the Austro-German border; to the south, looking into Italy, the Dolomites can be seen on the southern horizon; to the east are the mountains of the Venediger and Gross Glockner group embracing Austria's highest mountain; while close by is the frontier ridge leading to the Zillertal's highest peak across the glacial expanse of the Schwarzenstein to the Hochfeiler and beyond to the Oetztal and Stubai Alps.

*Summit cross on Grosser Loeffler, looking southwest along the Austro–Italian border*

On this route various mountaineering skills will be put to the test, particularly rope management and ice axe and crampon use, as a good number of crevasses will have to be jumped. The crevasses in the centre of the glacier are very deep and are not a place to contemplate crevasse rescue techniques. They need to be approached with the greatest care and respect. Once past the crevasse zone the demands of the route ease up slightly, with good scrambling over mixed ground to the summit.

In descent the same problems of route finding return to demand the uttermost attention, particularly as there is a greater risk of a fall or a slip. Again this calls for good rope management, with each participant keeping a respectful distance from their partner, so that if a fall does take place they do not go crashing into each other. Obviously this route should not be undertaken in less than fair weather or on a falling barometer, when route finding would be made difficult and dangerous in the extreme.

# STAGE 4
## Greizer Hut to the Berliner Hut

| | |
|---|---|
| **Start** | Greizer Hut (2226m) |
| **Finish** | Berliner Hut (2042m) |
| **Distance** | 8km |
| **Ascent** | 1220m |
| **Standard time** | 6–8hrs |
| **Note** | If you have youngsters with you, allow all day and be on your way by 07.00. |
| **Warning** | Some will find negotiating the ladder section intimidating. Note also that late winter snow on the west side of the Moerchen Scharte can be problematic if there is a lot of it. In bad weather, you would be advised to stay put in the Greizer Hut or to use the alternative route (see below) – descend to Ginzling (4hrs), then get the local bus service to Breitlahner and walk to the Berliner Hut (3hrs). This detour is not easy to accomplish in one day, and it maybe wiser if poor weather persists to overnight in Breitlahner or Ginzling before continuing. |

There are two options to choose from when deciding on your route from the Greizer Hut to the Berliner Hut. Stage 4 is the official Rucksack Route, while Stage 4a is a variant – a demanding alpine tour that takes in the Floitenkees glacier and Schwarzenstein Hut prior to descending to the Berliner Hut.

The early part of Stage 4 lacks any real views due to the loss of height immediately on leaving the hut. This situation is somewhat remedied on reaching a little saddle at 2287m, when good views re-establish themselves, with excellent scenery towards the Floitenkees glacier and around ▶

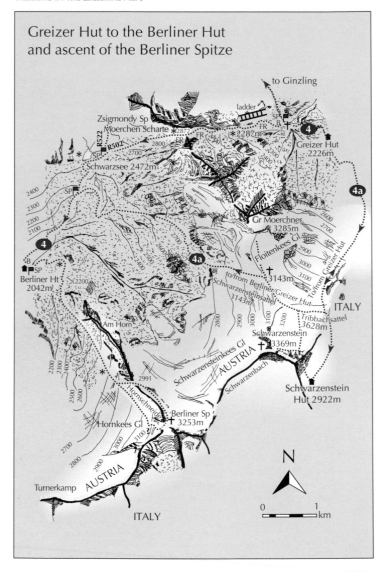

# Greizer Hut to the Berliner Hut
# and ascent of the Berliner Spitze

to Ginzling

ladder

SP

**4**

Greizer Hut
2226m

Zsigmondy Sp
Moerchen Scharte
*2872*
FR
*2287m* FR

R522
R502
SP
*2800*

Schwarzsee 2472m
*2700*

*2400*
*2300*
*2200*
*2100*

SP

**4a**

**4**

Gr Moerchner
3285m

*2600*
*2700*

Floitenkees Gl
*3000*
*3100*

to/from Greizer Hut

**4a**

B
SP
Berliner Ht
2042m

*2200*

to/from Berliner/Greizer Hut
Schwarzensteinsattel
3143m

*3143m*

ITALY

Am Horn

*2800*
*2900*
*3000*
*3100*
*3200*

Tribbachsattel
3628m

Schwarzenstein
3369m

*2200*
*2300*
*2400*
*2500*
*2600*

Schwarzensteinkees Gl
AUSTRIA
*2991*

Schwarzenbach

Schwarzenstein
Hut 2922m

Hornschneide

Berliner Sp
3253m

Hornkees Gl

*2700*
*2800*
*2900*
*3000*
*3100*

N

Turnerkamp
AUSTRIA

ITALY

0          1
|————————|
km

to the Grosser Loeffler and Schwarzenstein group. After that, the Moerchen Scharte provides a good mountaineering-type situation, as the col is located in a tight junction between the Grosser Moerchner's south ridge and the Rosskopfe, coming down from the Zsigmondy Spitze.

The walk down from the Moerchen Scharte is a truly splendid affair, particularly if you are blessed with good weather. The photo opportunities are excellent, and none more so than at the Schwarzsee lake and then just above the Berliner Hut, when the hut and Grosser Moseler are in view.

It is not often that the Zillertal Rucksack Route starts with a walk downhill, but this is how this today begins, and sadly well over 400m are lost in the initial stages, which have to be regained on the steep, muscle-tugging climb to the Moerchen Scharte.

From the **Greizer Hut**, descend west following signposts for Route 502 for the Berliner Hoehenweg and Berliner Hut, generally heading in the direction of the lovely village of Ginzling, and arrive a point at 1800m

*The route to the Moerchen Scharte as seen from the Greizer Hut*

The alternative poor weather route leaves the main route here.

where the route divides (1hr), with a signpost pointing the way to the Moerchen Scharte and the Berliner Hut, and down the valley to Ginzling. ◄ Cross open ground to the west through boulders and across glacial streams, some more torrent than babbling brook, frequently hindered by old snow and avalanche debris, to a footbridge to cross the raging torrents coming down from the Floitenkees glacier.

Continue west for a short distance to the foot of an obvious buttress and ridge coming down from the Moerchen Scharte. The track continues over rough ground – where route finding in this area is not always obvious due to avalanche debris, look for cairns and the usual daubs of red-paint route markers. The route as such then rises steeply, at which point you are confronted by a 6m high **ladder** followed by a series of **fixed ropes** to get round the buttress onto easier ground. This section is not hard, but it is exposed to some sizeable drops; those who are not entirely vertigo free should stay close to a companion, and everyone should make use of an improvised harness, as this is no place to risk a fall.

From here you can consider the plight of the light aircraft that crashed on the upper slope of the Grosser Loeffler in 1996.

The route now follows a track to and fro up the edge of the ridge to a small saddle noted as point 2287m on the AV map. This provides a much needed breathing space and is a good place to stop for a quick snack (there are no other suitable stopping places to rest until reaching the Moerchen Scharte). ◄ Try to work out the original route to and from the Greizer Hut, which made a contouring traverse across and around the then lower section of the Floitenkees glacier. Sadly the route no longer exists, no doubt blown away by avalanche, but it may be undertaken in winter by experienced ski-mountaineers.

Thereafter, at our modest level, the route continues steeply upward through a narrow couloir, aided in places by fixed wires, to exit at the obvious col that is the **Moerchen Scharte** (2872m) on the north ridge of the Grosser Moerchner (3285m, 3–4hrs). The col announces the end of the day's difficulties!

After being confined to steep slopes from the bottom of the Floitengrund valley to the top of the Moerchen

*Negotiating fixed ropes en route to the Moerchen Scharte and Berliner Hut*

Scharte, it is quite exhilarating on reaching the col to find that the route opens up to reveal a whole new range of mountains. Take time to review the panoramic view back towards the Greizer Hut, which is now isolated in an expanse of mountains that forms the frontier ridge with Italy, running in a wide arc from the Grosser Loeffler and around the great expanse of ice that forms the Floitenkees and Schwarzenstein glaciers. In the opposite direction, towards the southwest, is the route to the Furtschagl Haus across the Schoenbichler Scharte (3081m), the highest pass on the Zillertal Rucksack Route and the only pass over the magic height of 3000m.

From the col the descent route is obvious, with the Berliner Hut being about 2hrs away. Continue west, descending a steep track, rocky in parts, through an area known as the Rosskar, to the intersection with **Route 522** (heading north to the Max Hut via the Eissee and Melker Scharte) overlooking the tiny alpine lake of the **Schwarzsee** at 2472m. ◀

*If the weather is good, make the detour to the north shoreline for an excellent photo opportunity – with the Berliner Spitze and Horn Spitze group of mountains mirrored on the lake's surface.*

The track from here is a well-worn trail on a picturesque path that continues southwest on Route 502 over easy ground for a short hour to the very grand **Berliner Hut**.

### Alternative poor weather route

If you have bad weather while at the Greizer Hut and wish to continue with the tour, the following is a reluctant action plan. From the hut descend and follow the route description as far as the signpost pointing the way to the Moerchen Scharte and Berliner Hut. From here continue to descend the track until it widens into the forest service road and terminates at the Seilbahn material goods hoist for the hut. If you have played your cards right, you will have pre-booked the Floitental Shuttle Taxi Service (tel 0664 1029354) that will whisk you down the valley to Ginzling – or, even better, deposit you further up the valley at the Bergbauernhof Hotel at Breithlahner. ◀ Thereafter make the 3hr journey to the Berliner Hut, making a total journey time of about 6hrs. Should you opt to walk all the way to Ginzling this will take a minimum of 3hrs, plus time spent waiting for the local bus service, plus time taken walking to the Berliner Hut (see Hut directory, 'Berliner Hut', for bus times) making a very long day of around 8–9hrs.

*If the weather is foul you will not be the only ones hoping to reserve the shuttle service – book early to avoid disappointment!*

# STAGE 4A

*Greizer Hut to the Berliner Hut via the Floitenkees glacier or Schwarzenstein Hut*

| | |
|---|---|
| **Start** | Greizer Hut (2226m) |
| **Finish** | Berliner Hut (2042m) |
| **Distance** | 10km; or 12km via the Schwarzenstein Hut |
| **Ascent** | 1100m; or 1115m via the Schwarzenstein Hut |
| **Grade** | PD (for both routes) |
| **Standard time** | 6hrs; or 10hrs via the Schwarzenstein Hut |
| **Note** | See map Stages 4 and 4a. Undertake this route only in good clear weather as route finding on the Floitenkees glacier is extremely problematic and varies from year to year. Having crossed into Italy, you are committed to the route, as there is no easy way back into Austria. Should the weather turn bad you may be forced to have a prolonged stay in the South Tyrol or to descend into Italy and make a long, tedious return journey to Austria via Sterzing and the Brenner Pass. |
| **Warning** | Do not try this route after fresh snow fall – the crevasse dangers are very real without a carpet of snow adding to your difficulties. |

This is a first-class glacier journey, full of challenge and tremendous alpine scenery throughout. Those that climbed the Grosser Loeffler (Stage 3 excursion) will have the pleasure of seeing the mountain face on, with the labyrinth of crevasses seen to advantage. An overnight stop at the

Schwarzenstein Hut will put an extra day onto the basic itinerary, but if you and your companions are aspirant alpinists and looking to add that little extra spice to your Bergtour (and if the weather is good), then this glacial route comes highly recommended. Fit, strong parties may cut out the Schwarzenstein Hut and make a direct journey to the Berliner Hut in about 6 hours if conditions are good. Everyone else can just enjoy the high ambience of the Schwarzenstein Hut's airy perch.

Before setting out from the hut, ask the guardian whether the route is marked. Also, if your group is small, enquire if there are other groups making the same journey to provide strength in numbers should a mishap occur.

◄ From the **Greizer Hut**, follow the obvious track heading southeast towards the **Floitenkees glacier**. The track rises steeply in a series of steps over rocks and boulders to reach the glacier at 2600m. Look for marker poles and tracks, as the route varies from year to year. Gear up and ensure Prusik loops are in place and all other tackle accessible should you need it (1hr).

Get onto the glacier, setting a course to cross the glacier in a wide arc. First, head south to a point below the Ostliches Floiten Spitze peak. Then make an oblique traverse left to right, passing the foot of the Westlicher Floiten Spitze. Cross the heavily crevassed glacial basin, taking extra care hereabouts, heading west for the obvious rock buttress coming down from the Felskopfl on the 3000m contour (2hrs).

There is now a choice of route – either to head for the Berliner Hut or to overnight at the Schwartzenstein Hut.

### To continue to the Berliner Hut

Head west through the upper snowfields and rocky outcrops, climbing steadily through the rocks to point 3140m on the AV map, from where the upper reaches of the glacier flatten out below the Feldkopfl. In good conditions, strong parties may climb the very steep upper snow slope direct, keeping right (north), avoiding the traverse through the rocks (1hr). The route now joins up with the route from the Berliner Hut.

Descend the rounded snow rib northwest, bypassing crevasses to point 3143m on the Schwarzensteinsattel (saddle), midway across the glacier at the foot of the

Grosser Moerchner's south ridge. From here a quick 1hr round-trip detour may be made to the summit of the Moerchner before vacating the gleaming glacier slopes for the Berliner Hut. From the saddle, descend the **Schwarzensteinkees glacier** in a westerly direction; beware of crevasses midway and head for a rocky island (*rognon*) at 2945m. Get off the glacier and scramble down rocks (some with wires) and one gully fitted with a short ladder, then head across patches of snow to reach easy ground (2hrs). The route is waymarked from here, and descends a rocky trail through the Moerchenkar boulder field to eventually meet up with the normal route over the Moerchen Scharte at point 2256m (1hr) to arrive at the **Berliner Hut**.

*Route to the Berliner Hut via the Tribbachsattel and Schwarzenstein Hut*

### To continue to the Schwarzenstein Hut

From the 3000m contour, head south and take a direct path to the obvious snowy plateau that is the **Tribbachsattel** saddle at 3028m on the Austrian–Italian ridge. ▶ From the col/saddle, the Schwarzenstein Hut is clearly visible on the rocky rib of the Tribbachschneide ridge some 100m below. Continue down the right bank

Look out for a very large signpost that marks the border.

of the Tribbachkees glacier to a point below the hut, and then simply scramble up rocks to the superbly sited **Schwarzenstein Hut** (2922m, 1hr).

In reverse, and to continue to the Berliner Hut, first climb the rocks at the back of the **Schwarzenstein Hut** then climb a steepish snowfield that leads to the summit of the Felskopfl (3235m) at the southern tip of the Schwarzenstein's east ridge (1hr+). To join up with the route to the Berliner Hut simply head northwest across the glacier to the Schwarzensteinsattel at 3143m.

Alternatively, suitably inspired aplinists may wish to make a highly recommended 1hr detour and bag the **Schwarzenstein** peak (3369m) by traversing the mountain via the frontier ridge before descending to the Berliner Hut. This route provides excellent views across the entire Zillertal and of the South Tyrol to the Riesenferner Group and beyond to the Dolomites.

# EXCURSION 4.1

*Ascent of the Berliner Spitze (Horn Spitze III)*
*(3253m)*

| | |
|---|---|
| **Start** | Berliner Hut |
| **Distance** | 4km |
| **Ascent** | 1215m |
| **Grade** | PD |
| **Standard ascent time** | 4–5hrs |
| **Note** | Hot, moist air coming from the south soon starts to build cloud by mid-morning making the descent from the summit and across the glacier more problematic. It is advisable to be on your way early and out of the hut for 06.00. |

This is an excellent climb over mixed ground on a popular peak, all of which is visible from the Berliner Hut's terrace. The climb is much more sporting than the normal route, and provides that much needed experience for aspirant alpinists to differentiate between routes that are graded Easy or Facile and those graded Moderately Difficult or Peu Difficile. (This route is graded PD, mostly because of the rock climbing involved.)

The approach to the climb is excellent, with scenic interest being provided by the dominant wedge of Turnerkamp's north face, a mountain having no easy route to the top. Once walkers are off the Hornkees glacier and onto the ridge the feeling of open space is superb with fine alpine scenery in all directions – particularly towards the glacial expanse of the Schwarzenstien glacier. This continues to improve, and is bettered only on the summit.

From the **Berliner Hut** proceed east following the path below the hut to get across the Zemmbach stream (signpost for the Berliner Spitze). The track continues east heading for the obvious long northwest ridge coming down from the Horn Spitze. Climb the rock buttress in a series of long looping zigzags through dwarf alpine rose and juniper bushes, over slabs and rocky ground, until the route turns southeast below the **Am Horn** to follow the general line of the Hornschneide ridge (signpost) (20mins).

Proceed over rocks and boulders in a rising traverse, sometimes on paved slabs that have been painstakingly laid out, then midway, in total contrast, the track heads through a series of rock falls with huge boulders and ankle-twisting terrain until they eventually peter out when the track meets the **Hornkees glacier** on the 2800m contour (2hrs).

Get onto the glacier and continue southeast on the north edge of the right bank heading for a rock island immediately below an obvious col on the ridge above. From hereabouts, on the 2900m contour turn left (east) to climb the steep snow slope, taking care to avoid the obvious crevasse zone, before finally scrambling up the rocks to reach the col at **2991m**. ▸ There are excellent

It is advisable to climb the steeper sections of the snow slope in a series of pitches, as the fall line is directly above some crevasses.

*On the Hornkees glacier with Turnerkamp (3420m) on the left; Grosser Moseler (3480m) to the right dominates the frontier ridge with the South Tyrol. There are no easy routes on these mountains.*

mountain situations from here on, should you be blessed by good weather (3hrs).

From the col, scramble and climb along the obvious ridge line as directly as possible. The ridge rises in a series of steps, with the steeper sections graded around the rock climbing standard of Difficult Grade III, and these can be turned left or right to eventually emerge on the **Berliner Spitze** summit at 3253m, with its large wooden cross (4–5hrs). The summit provides the opportunity to see over the other side of the mountain deep into Italy and the South Tyrol, with the jagged peaks of the Dolomites breaking the skyline on the southern horizon, then look more closely along the frontier ridge to Turnerkamp and the lofty summits of the Grosser Moseler and Hochfeiler.

*If you took your crampons off to climb the ridge and traverse the mountain, now is a good time to put them back on again!*

From the summit proceed to descend south over mixed ground for a short distance until an obvious gully system is reached. Descend this, moving cautiously over steep rock and snow, taking care to use in-situ belays when moving together. Exit the rocks onto the upper reaches of the **Hornkees glacier** prior to descending the glacier to a point just north of the Mittebachjoch. ◄

Descend the glacier by reversing the normal route up the mountain, which in summer is often a well-beaten snowy trail. Proceed by heading northwest on the glacier's upper right bank, descending steeply, with attendant but obvious crevasse danger in the mid-sections. Negotiate this to exit at the starting point on the rocky moraine at 2800m.

From this point, reverse the journey back to the **Berliner Hut**. But be warned – do not attempt to make a short cut and detour below the Am Horn back to the hut, as there are several steep rock faces to negotiate, remnants left long ago by the retreating Hornkees glacier.

The climb up the snow slope to get onto the ridge proper can be problematic late in season with minimal snow cover. The upper slopes are frequently iced and are better climbed in a series of pitches rather than, as is the norm, moving together. The fall line lies above a series of crevasses, which could easily swallow a horse and cart let alone a hapless climber. Care on this section cannot be overstressed.

In descent from the summit be careful when climbing down the gully system. On the steeper sections these should be reversed and downclimbed in a series of short pitches to place running belays to get onto the glacier.

*Schwarzsee with the Berliner Spitze 3253m in the distance*

# STAGE 5
## Berliner Hut to the Furtschagl Haus

| | |
|---|---|
| **Start** | Berliner Hut (2042m) |
| **Finish** | Furtschagl Haus (2295m) |
| **Distance** | 8km |
| **Ascent** | 1041m |
| **Standard time** | 6–7hrs |
| **Note** | With over 1000m of uphill to negotiate and a high pass to cross, you need to be on your way early, preferably no later than 07.00. |
| **Warning** | There are difficulties in negotiating the steep sections on both sides of the Schoenbichler Scharte, the upper sections of which usually retain a fair amount of old hard-packed snow. Both sides of the pass have fixed ropes to aid stability; the ground is very steep and not that good underfoot, and use of the fixed ropes is essential when carrying a big rucksack. Use your long sling and karabiner to make an improvised rudimentary harness. |

This is an excellent alpine journey, and although not unduly difficult it navigates the highest pass on the Rucksack Route, the Schoenbichler Scharte, the only pass over 3000m. The route has excellent scenic interest throughout, particularly around the 2500m contour, where the panoramic backdrop to the Berliner Hut and Moerchen Scharte is particularly fine.

Thereafter, the scene is dominated in ascent by the Grosser Moseler, then in descent by the Zillertal's highest peak, the Hochfeiler. From the top of the Schoenbichler Horn the scene is a stunning array of wall-to-wall mountains.

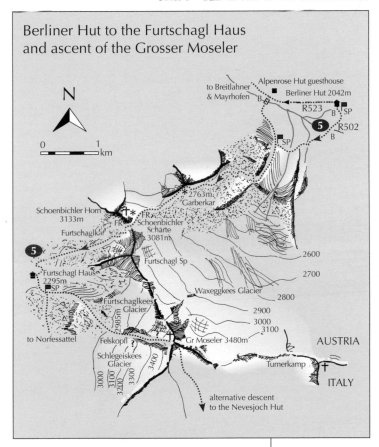

# Berliner Hut to the Furtschagl Haus and ascent of the Grosser Moseler

From the **Berliner Hut**, continue to follow the familiar signs for Route 502 for the Berliner–Zillertal Hoehenweg (also known as the Central Alpine Way). Cross the footbridge a little way below the hut to get across the raging torrents of the Zammbach river, heading southwest to a second footbridge. The path follows a well-defined trail that contours around grassy slopes and rock outcrops as it heads for a subsidiary ridge coming down from the

Garberkar and a junction with the path heading north to the Alpenrose Hut guest house (1hr) (signpost).

From here the track pitches up, with the ground starting to rise more steeply to follow glacial debris through an open couloir that forms the **Garberkar**. Follow the rocky slopes to 2600m and the junction with the track that heads south onto the Waxeggkees glacier. ◄  Sharp eyes will be able to pick out the track leading across the glacier to the Moseler Scharte.

Continue southwest, hugging the ridge, with the track rising in a series of steep zigzags over wearisome, difficult ground of rock, shale and scree, all mixed in with patches of snow. The path of sorts rises more steeply at the top, where for the last 100m you are aided by fixed wire ropes, to emerge on the rocky **Schoenbichler Scharte** at 3081m, where you will be greeted with great views of the Hochfeiler's north face and beyond, with a whole new set of mountain scenery to enjoy (about 4½hrs).

From the col, it is possible to make a 5mins excursion and scramble up the final steep rocky slopes to the summit of the **Schoenbichler Horn** (3133m) to obtain even better views of the adjacent Grosser Moseler, the

*Excellent views of the Waxeggkees glacier and the north flank of the Grosser Moseler.*

*The magnificent Berliner Hut*

*Negotiating steep difficult ground, aided by fixed ropes, at the Schoenbichler Scharte en route to the Furtschagl Haus*

glacial expanse of the Hochfeiler, and across the void to the Olperer, as well as (looking back) to the Grosser Loeffler, with an opportunity to review the whole journey so far.

▶ From the col descend steeply, zigzagging to and fro to get round the steep rocks, patches of snow, loose rocks and shale, with fixed wires in place on the steeper sections, until the ground gradually eases on the 2700m contour.

In descent, the upper section of the Schoenbichler Scharte is frequently covered with hard snow for the first 50m or so. Take care!

With the hut in view, continue southwest, now on easier ground, down the ridge of an old glacial moraine, zigzagging through the **Furtschaglkar** boulder field while enjoying the excellent views of the Grosser Moseler and north face of the Hochfeiler and on to the **Furtschagel Haus** (about 2hrs from the col).

This is not a route to do in poor weather, when route finding becomes increasingly problematic; in heavy rain the top of the Schoenbichler Scharte runs with water, and in a thunderstorm the wire ropes zing with electricity. In bad weather walkers on a tight schedule can to descend to Breitlahner and get the bus to Schlegeis, omitting the Furtschagl Haus, and then take the short walk to the congenial Olperer Hut (see Stage 6).

# EXCURSION 5.1

*Ascent of the Grosser Moseler (3480m)*
*via the west spur*

| | |
|---|---|
| **Start** | Furtschagl Haus |
| **Distance** | 3km |
| **Ascent** | 1187m |
| **Grade** | PD |
| **Standard ascent time** | 4–5hrs |
| **Note** | Be on your way early – breakfast at 05.30 and out of the door for 06.00. As usual, the route should be avoided in less than good settled weather. |

Perhaps the most challenging of mountains on the Rucksack Route, this is a magnificent day out up the Zillertal's second highest, and perhaps most scenic mountain. The route climbs the mountain by the west spur through stunning scenery and provides an opportunity to descend into Italy for those who wish to undertake parts of the Zillertal South Tyrol Tour.

The summit is a true summit, being steep on all sides and invoking that feeling that you have climbed to the top of something very special. From it, there are excellent views in all directions.

From the **Furschagl Haus** follow signs for the mountain, proceeding first downhill to cross the Furtschaglbach river then heading uphill for 20mins following signposts for the Norfessattel pass on the Italian border and your objective, the Grosser Moseler.

The route now turns southeast, climbing steadily up a ridge of glacial moraine with some large stone cairns to point 2727m and the junction with the **Schlegeiskees glacier**. Tackle up and get onto the glacier, heading east to the foot of an obvious buttress. Cross the glacier, keeping below the ice fall and avoiding several lines of crevasses en route.

Round the buttress until an obvious gully and tight couloir come into view. Make for this, climbing steepish snow slopes. Negotiate the Bergschrund and get onto the rocky rib on the right-hand side (2¾hrs).

Climb the rocks to the right-hand side of the couloirs that steepen considerably at the top, with short pitches of moderate to difficult, to exit on the summit snowfield. Stone marker cairns exist but are not consistent. The summit is obvious from here on, with its large wooden cross in clear sight. Climb and cross the snowfield, which is steep in places, heading for a notch to the left of the summit followed by a short exposed corniced ridge to the top of **Grosser Moseler** with its large wooden cross (4½hrs).

The panoramic view from the summit is extensive in all directions, particularly along the frontier ridge towards Turnerkamp and the Schwarzenstein, where some crevasses of gigantic proportions maybe seen. Then, in the opposite direction, across the great swathe of glacier lies the classic north face of the Hochfeiler, with close neighbour Hoher Weisszint.

*The route up from the Furschagl Haus*

Looking east along the frontier ridge – Austria on the left, Italy and the South Tyrol on the right, with the triangular wedge of Turnerkamp (3420m) in the distance. The small col immediately ahead to the right leads to the Nevesjoch Hut.

The **first ascent** of Grosser Moseler from the south was by a British party of Fox, Freshfield, Tuckett (Alpine Club), and French guides Francois Davouassoud and Peter Michel on a rare visit to the Eastern Alps on 16 June 1865. They reached Zamseralm at 7pm, almost coming to grief several times in the dark.

In descent reverse the route in its entirety. Take time to look over the northwest face, which has extreme breath-taking vertical exposure together with some tremendous ice cliffs, hanging glaciers and gigantic crevasses. Exercise care and time while descending the rocky rib, remembering to place running belays on the steeper sections. Similar care is needed when reversing the Bergschrund. Thereafter, the rest of the journey should be a pleasant stroll back to the **Furschagl Haus**.

The crux of the main route is in negotiating the steep rocky rib of the Felskopfl. This is comprised of slabs of rock and flakes on edge; it is very steep, with the odd places close to vertical, but fortunately these sections are short (4–6m in length). There is plenty of opportunity to belay and climb safely.

Some parties do climb the stone couloir direct, but note that this acts as a stone chute of sorts and, unless absolutely, necessary should be avoided due to the risk of falling stones, particularly late in the day when parties are coming off the mountain and people are more likely to dislodge rocks. More recently parties have started to climb the buttress to the far left of the couloir, but this also is quite loose at the top.

### Alternative descent to Nevesjoch Hut

For those aspirant alpinists who have ambitions to climb the Hochfeiler, climbing the Grosser Moseler and descending from the summit into the South Tyrol will provide that opportunity by descending to Nevesjoch Hut. Apart from the initial stages the descent route to the Nevesjoch Hut is more straightforward than the ascent from Furtschagl Haus, being entirely on rock, apart from patches of snow (allow 3–4hrs). (See ZSTT Excursion 5.1.)

## STAGE 6
*Furtschagl Haus to the Olperer Hut*

| | |
|---|---|
| **Start** | Furtschagl Haus (2295m) |
| **Finish** | Olperer Hut (2388m) |
| **Distance** | 9km; 10.5km via scenic route |
| **Ascent** | 590m (both routes) |
| **Standard time** | 5–6hrs; 7–8hrs via scenic route |

This is quite an easy day's tour compared to the previous day's outings, and the second one on the clockwise tour of the Rucksack Route to start off downhill. However, despite this relative ease, it is still a long way to the Olperer Hut, and most groups will take 5hrs to complete the journey.

On leaving the Furtschagl Haus the views of the Grosser Moseler and Hochfeiler are lost, but are soon replaced with a splendid view of the Olperer, third highest peak in the Zillertal, which occupies the attention up to the tourist rest area at Zamsgatterl–Jausenstat. Here, if the weather is good and you are feeling strong, take the long way to the Olperer Hut via the highly recommended scenic route.

The main route continues with an easy walk along the edge of the Schlegeisspeicher reservoir, with its forest fringe, which makes a pleasant change from the previous day's outings on the high peak. However, the real reward of the day is the splendid Olperer Hut, with its delightful terrace and extensive panoramic view across the Schlegeisspeicher to the Grosser Moseler and Hochfeiler. What better way to rest and relax after a day's walk than to have a pleasant meal and a drink overlooking such fine scenery – excellent!

From **Furtschagl Haus** pick up the trail once more of the Berliner–Zillertal Hoehenweg. As a change from the high-level route of previous days, the route starts by descending steeply following the **Central Alpine Way** of Route 502. Then more steep zigzags lead to an easy path northeast to the tip of the man-made lake that is the **Schlegeisspeicher** hydro-electric reservoir.

While wandering along the shores of the **Schlegeisspeicher reservoir**, with its 130m high dam wall, it is worthwhile pondering the fate of the various buildings and alms that were flooded to make way for progress and the provision of

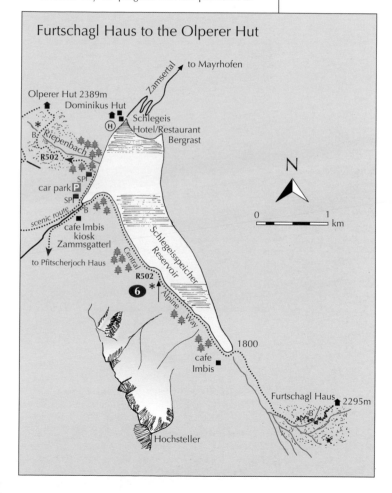

## Furtschagl Haus to the Olperer Hut

to Mayrhofen

Zamsertal

Olperer Hut 2389m
Dominikus Hut
Schlegeis Hotel/Restaurant Bergrast

Riepenbach

R502

car park

SP

SP

scenic route

cafe Imbis kiosk Zammsgatterl

to Pfitscherjoch Haus

R502

6

Schlegeisspeicher Reservoir

Central

Alpine Way

1800

cafe Imbis

Furtschagl Haus 2295m

Hochsteller

N

0          1
km

The Olperer (3476m), as seen from the Schlegeisspeicher reservoir en route to the Olperer Hut (circled), with the snowy arete of the Schneegupf and Gefrorne Wand Spitze (right)

hydro-electricity. One such place was the original Dominikus Hut, which was constructed as a private venture by members of the OeAV Sektion Prague in 1883. The hut was named after the original Huettenwirt, Herr Dominikus. It should be remembered that at that time, just getting to the upper reaches of the Zamsergrund valley was in itself a major expedition, and the Dominikus Hut provided much needed accommodation midway.

In 1971 the Schlegeis hyro-electric project was completed; the valley was flooded and the original

Dominikus Hut was lost forever. A new privately owned hut was built high above the reservoir as recompense for loss of the old hut, to cater for the many daytime visitors that now congregate in the area, and its white-fronted gable end can be seen from across the lake. A journey which 100 years ago would have taken a day's hard slog is now covered in less than an hour by bus from Mayrhofen railway station.

The route then follows a single-track graded service road, with good views towards the Olperer and Hoeher Riffler, which traverses along the base of the Kleiner Hochsteller adjacent to the lake's left bank for 3.5km. Walkers who have ambitions of climbing the Olperer (see ascent details below) should take good note as the route is clearly seen, particularly the Schneegupf snow arête, from the edge of the lake. Similarly, the route from the Olperer Hut to Friesenberg Haus (Stage 7) is well defined, since both huts are clearly visible to the eagle-eyed. The road arrives at a large car park at **Zamsgatterl–Jausenstat**, complete with rest area, cafeterias, restaurant and all the trappings of tourism (2hrs). ▶

Despite the commercialism, this is a relatively pleasant place to stop and take an extended breather and perhaps get something to eat before leaving for loftier places.

## OTHER ROUTE OPTIONS

For those walkers with time on their hands, a one-day detour can be made from Zamsgatterl–Jausenstat by heading for the Italian border for an overnight stay at the Pfitscherjoch Haus (2277m) at the head of the Zamsergrund valley. Then follow Route 528 towards the Geraer Hut and Alpeiner Scharte before turning off to follow the route to the Olperer Hut (see Stage 6a).

Similarly, for aspirant alpinist this is a good place to peel away from the main Zillertal valley and head for Pfitscherjoch and the South Tyrol, extending the tour by five days for some top-notch hut-to-hut tours and brilliant peaks. (This route joins the ZSTT at Stage 2.)

At Zamsgatterl–Jausenstat there is a choice of routes to the Olperer Hut – take either the normal (and shortest) way or the 1hr longer scenic route (described below).

*The Hochfeiler (3510m), highest peak in the Zillertal*

For the normal way to the Olperer Hut, continue north along the road in the direction of Mayrhofen overlooking the reservoir to the **Schlegeis Restaurant**, and a little further find a signpost indicating the way uphill to the Dominikus and Olperer Huts.

Proceed northwest, climbing steeply following a good path through forest and alpine rose bushes, zigzagging over blocks along a well-defined trail to a point on the 2300m contour and footbridge across the **Riepenbach** glacial stream.

There is good scenery hereabouts back across the void towards the Furtschagl Haus, the Grosser Moseler and the huge ice wall of the Hochferner and Hochfeiler. Cross the stream and continue to follow the path easily to the **Olperer Hut** (a short 3hrs from Zamsgatterl–Jausenstat).

**Scenic route to the Olperer Hut**
Alternatively, at the Imbis cafe kiosk at **Zamsgatterl** and the Schlegeis car park area find the junction of all paths including the track to Pfitscherjoch, where there is a signpost indicating the way to the Olperer Hut by

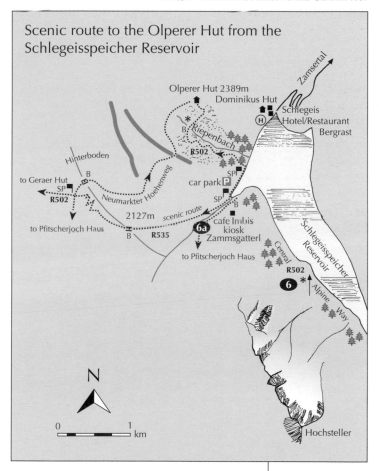

## Scenic route to the Olperer Hut from the Schlegeisspeicher Reservoir

Zamsertal

Olperer Hut 2389m
Dominikus Hut
Schlegeis Hotel/Restaurant
Bergrast

B. Riepenbach

R502

Hinterboden

to Geraer Hut
SP
R502

B

Neumarkter Hoehenweg

SP

car park P

SP
B

2127m    scenic route

to Pfitscherjoch Haus

B    R535

6a

cafe Imbis
kiosk
Zammsgatterl

to Pfitscherjoch Haus

Central

Schlegeisspeicher Reservoir

R502

6

Alpine Way

N

0        1
            km

Hochsteller

the Neumarkter Runde Panorama Hoehenweg. This route will add an extra hour to the time, but is far more rewarding than the voie normal as it has excellent scenery throughout, particularly in the latter part of the walk, which offers exceptional views across the Schlegeis reservoir towards the high peaks.

Pick up the track as directed, following **Route 535** southwest along a well-constructed path through the forest, with rhododendron and dwarf alpine pine bushes, for around 1hr to a footbridge across the Unterschrammachbach glacial river at 2127m. Cross the river and follow the track now more steeply northwest into the large open combe and glacial basin of **Hinterboden** (about 1½hrs). There is a signpost for Pfitscherjoch Haus, Geraer Hut and Olperer Hut.

Bear right (north), now on Route 502, better known as the **Central Alpine Way**, rounding the head of the combe to gain the rocky slopes of Schramerkopf. Follow the obvious rocky trail by traversing around the hillside below Schramerkopf on a path that has been painstakingly laid out (being part-paved in places) until its conclusion at the **Olperer Hut** (3hrs).

# STAGE 6A
*Furtschagl Haus to the Olperer Hut via Pfitscherjoch Haus*

| | |
|---|---|
| **Start** | Furtschagl Haus (2295m) |
| **Finish** | Olperer Hut (2389m), with overnight stay at Pfitscherjoch Haus (2277m) |
| **Distance** | 12.5km |
| **Ascent** | 480m |
| **Standard time** | Day 1: 4–5hrs; Day 2: 6hrs |
| **Note** | After wet weather the streams can be quite ferocious, with the marshy areas being particularly wet. If it's pouring with rain walkers are advised to take the easy route back down the valley to Schlegeis and from there to follow the normal route to the Olperer Hut (see Stage 6). |

This is a fine two-day alternative route to the Olperer Hut that provides some very good scenery down the Zamsergrund valley towards Schlegeis, then offers more on the Neuemarkter Runde Panorama Hoehenweg with its views across the Schlegeissspeicher reservoir. The Pfitscherjoch Haus provides an overnight stay, and anyone with an interest in the relics of war should take some time to explore the old army buildings and trench systems just to the south of the hut.

Follow the route from Furtschagl Haus to the car park and rest area at **Zamsgatterl-Jausenstat** (see Stage 6). From here, pick up the trail for this ancient trading route and follow **Route 524**, heading southwest along a single-track graded road. This follows the right bank of the Zamserbach river for 5km along the Via Alpina trail for 2hrs to Pfitscherjoch, the border with Italy and the province of Sudtyrol, and eventually to **Pfitscherjoch Haus** and hut (4–5hrs) for an overnight stay.

The next day, from the hut head north and return to the border crossing that was passed the previous day, with the old border police customs hut and roadside chapel. At the pass, continue down the single-track road noted as Hochettleck for around 500m to where the track turns to head down the valley (signpost). Here strike off left picking up the trail heading northwest on **Route 528**, initially descending across open marshy ground of Stampler Boden to a footbridge and area where many streams congregate (some of which are quite strong and aggressive).

The route now turns more northeasterly to progress across the open boulder slopes of the **Die Lenzen**, **Wantler** and **Ebenler**, making a rising traverse over rocky ground – some of which has been painstakingly laid out and paved – until it rounds the foot of the Kastenschneid ridge at 2394m, where there is a large stone **cairn**.

The route now turns left (northwest) to round the **Oberschrammachkar** couloir and boulder field on the 2400m contour, with a second large purpose-built stone **cairn** at the foot of the Ameiskopf ridge (2465m). Rounding the ridge the track comes to a sudden halt after 500m with a large signpost noting that the way ahead is

# Furtschagl Haus to the Olperer Hut via the Pfitscherjoch Haus

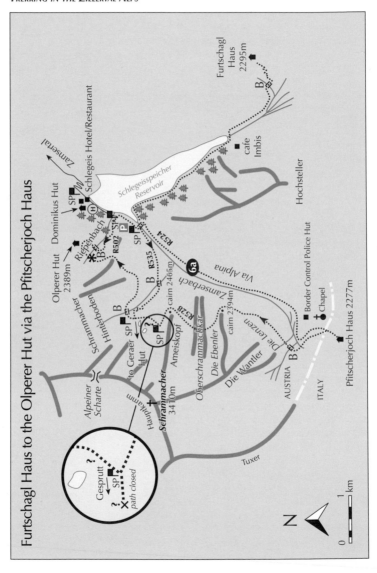

CURT
MAR

xxxxxx9008

Exp: 2/22/2023

Item: 0010079998489
796.51094 H2551T

CRUT
MAR
xxxxxxxx9008
Exb: 21551503
Item: 00107999489
Tras1H4S5ff1

Printed: Tuesday, February 14, 2023

'Gesprutt' and closed (about 3hrs). This marks the end of the original route, which changed irrevocably due to a massive rock fall in 2002 that totally obliterated the track to the Geraer and Olperer Huts. This point is approximately half-way, but easier ground lies ahead.

At the signpost turn right and descend the rocky slope north to the open marshy ground of **Hinterboden**, passing a number of small ponds to reach the junction of Route 535, with the new Neuemarkter Runde Panorama Hoehenweg footpath coming up the valley from Schlegeis (½hr) (signpost).

Traverse the open marshy ground and cross the Unterschrammachbach glacial stream, ascending the rocky slope immediately above to the 2350m contour. From here the route is obvious to the **Olperer Hut** (2hrs). ▶

This path was constructed by the DAV Sektion Neuemarkt in 2006 as an alternative and more scenic route to the Olperer Hut.

# EXCURSION 6.1
*Ascent of the Olperer (3476m)*

| | |
|---|---|
| **Start** | Olperer Hut |
| **Distance** | 3km |
| **Ascent** | 1100m |
| **Grade** | PD |
| **Standard ascent time** | 4–5hrs |

This is an excellent climb via the Schneegupf southeast ridge over mixed ground with some exhilarating situations. This is the third highest peak in the Zillertal (first ascent by A von Bohm and brothers E and O Zsigmondy in 1879), and despite the scrappy approach it provides a fine mountaineering route full of good alpine situations. The climb itself does not really get going until you reach the rocky platform of sorts at the foot of the Schneegupf snowfield. Thereafter the climb is superb, particularly if you are blessed with good weather – the climb up the Schneegupf snow arête to gain the summit rocks is a classic alpine snow ridge, with an airy if somewhat intimidating view across the Olperer's north face. The scramble over the summit rocks is exciting stuff, with breath-taking scenery tempered with equally breath-taking drops with heaps of exposure.

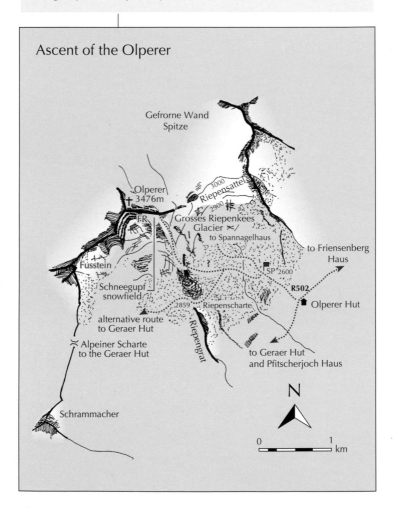

Ascent of the Olperer

Gefrorne Wand Spitze

Riepensattel
3000

Olperer
† 3476m

Grosses Riepenkees Glacier
2900
to Spannagelhaus

F.R.

to Friensenberg Haus

Fusstein

SP 2600

R502

Schneegupf snowfield

Olperer Hut

2859  Riepenscharte

alternative route to Geraer Hut

Riepengrat

Alpeiner Scharte to the Geraer Hut

to Geraer Hut and Pfitscherjoch Haus

Schrammacher

N

0          1
          km

From the **Olperer Hut**, the route starts off immediately uphill, heading northwest following a well-defined zig-zagging trail in the tracks of the old route to the Geraer Hut via the Alpeiner Scharte on Route 502 of the Central Alpine Way. ▶ Continue through the Riepenkar Couloir heading for the intersection with the track over the snow slopes of the now dormant Riepenkees glacier to the Spannagelhaus (½hr) (signpost for the Olperer).

At this intersection, continue as before for another ¾hr, making a rising traverse bearing left (west) through difficult ground of large blocks and boulders, where route finding is not always obvious. Look out for stone cairns, but generally head for a notch on the south ridge immediately above the Riepenscharte at point 2864m on the lower section of the Riepengrat ridge coming down from the Olperer's south ridge (1¼hrs) (signpost for the Olperer).

Pick a way through the rocks, scrambling over difficult mixed ground of large boulders and patches of snow, heading in a northerly direction – with the objective being simply to get onto the ridge. There are some stone cairns in places, but these are not frequent and

This route was redirected in 2006 due to severe earth tremors that resulted in massive rock falls to the east of the Alpeiner Scharte, making the route unsafe.

*Route marked, with the Schneegupf snow arête clearly seen and the Olperer Hut circled*

*Progressing through
fixed wires on the
summit ridge*

Excellent scenery
across the whole of
the Zillertal and near
peaks of the Olperer
and Fusstein.

obvious, with the result that there are quite a few false trails. Once on the ridge, continue to climb following the natural line of the ridge, turning difficult sections left or right. The ridge is guarded at its head by a much steeper rock outcrop. Scramble through the rocks of the headwall that leads eventually to a platform-cum-terrace on the lower edge of the **Schneegupf snowfield** (1hr; total time about 2–2½hrs). This is a good place to take a short break and to investigate the route, as the summit is clearly seen from here. ◄

From hereon the route is pretty obvious. Climb the steep snowfield and head for the snow arête and ridge on the northern skyline, keeping left on the south side if the ridge is corniced; otherwise climb the ridge direct. Continue along the snow crest, heading for the rocks coming down from the summit. ▶

Traverse around the base of the rocks to gain a chimney, fitted out with Klettersteige-style steel cables, spikes and staples for aid. Clip into the gear provided and climb the chimney direct to gain the ridge. Continue along the ridge (very exposed in places), climbing the rocks until stopped by a tower just below the summit. Gingerly bypass the tower on the right (north) and exit over a small narrow snowfield to gain the Olperer's somewhat small summit with sculptured metal cross (2hrs).

The near views from the summit, particularly of the rocky Fusstein, are truly superb. Across the void are visible the snow-capped peaks of the Grosser Loeffler, Moseler and Hochfeiler; further to the east on the far horizon the Gross Venediger and Gross Glockner show themselves; while to the south are the jagged peaks of the Dolomites.

In descent the route has to be reversed in its entirety. This demands a little extra care when passing the rock tower and down-climbing the rock chimney; for a group of people it is quicker to rig an abseil rope. Similarly, when descending the steepish snow arête, when the snow will be less than ideal, participants should keep themselves reasonably well spaced out to check a fall should the need arise.

Good views across the Olperer's northern flank to the Gefrorne Wand Spitze, with its attendant summer ski slopes, and the great bulk of the rocky Fusstein (3380m), even if it is something of a slag heap!

The main difficulties on the mountain are with route finding. First, you need to find your way through the maze of boulders on the upper Riepenkar to get onto the ridge and route (then to do it again in reverse to get off it). Thereafter, once on the climb, the difficulties are obvious and well defined. On the snow arête avoid the cornice if there is one, more so early in season, and then on the summit rocks place running belays at the difficult sections when moving together. Needless to say, this is not a climb to do in less than favourable weather or to undertake on a falling barometer.

# STAGE 7

*Olperer Hut to Friesenberg Haus*

| | |
|---|---|
| **Start** | Olperer Hut (2388m) |
| **Finish** | Friesenberg Haus (2477m) |
| **Distance** | 4km |
| **Ascent** | 580m |
| **Standard time** | 2½hrs |
| **Note** | Take care when descending the gully system and rock buttress that overlooks the hut and Friesenberg See. This is made more problematic when patches of snow linger on the rock ledges and steep sections. The less sure-footed should stay close to a companion for assistance and make good use of trekking poles. |

While somewhat short on duration, this is a very pleasant half-day outing traverses high above the Zamsergrund valley and offers excellent views across the valley towards Schlegeis and, a little later, to the triangular wedge of the Hoeher Riffler.

From the **Olperer Hut**, with signpost just outside the front door, follow **Route 526** on the Berliner Hoehenweg. The route starts off on a good track, and after 5mins or so a suspension bridge is reached to cross a washed-out gully – lasting evidence of the rock fall and mud avalanche that tore the back off the former hut in 1998 in one single destructive stroke, an event that forced to hut to close for a season and perhaps sealed the fate of the fine old hut. Thereafter the route traverses rocks and grassy slopes on an easygoing good path, generally on the 2500m contour, bypassing the Gefrorne Wand Spitze's east flank and the rocks of the **Gamsleiten**.

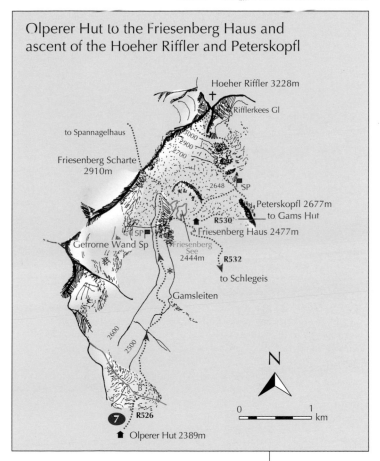

## Olperer Hut to the Friesenberg Haus and ascent of the Hoeher Riffler and Peterskopfl

Hoeher Riffler 3228m

Rifflerkees Gl

to Spannagelhaus

3000
2900
2700

Friesenberg Scharte
2910m

2648    SP

Peterskopfl 2677m

R530    to Gams Hut

Friesenberg Haus 2477m

SP

Gefrorne Wand Sp

Friesenberg
See
2444m    R532

to Schlegeis

Gamsleiten

2600
2500

N

0    1
km

7    R526

Olperer Hut 2389m

Once past the Gamsleiten, the path makes a rising traverse north, which eventually leads to a junction with a high-level track that leads to the clearly visible Friesenberg Scharte at 2910m (1+hrs) (signpost). Excellent views towards the peak of the Hoeher Riffler – those with sharp eyes will be able to pick out many of the stone cairns on top of the little peak of Peterskopfl.

*Hoeher Riffler with unseasonal snow covering en route to the Friesenberg Haus – the hut is visible to the right of the tiny alpine lake of Friesenberg See*

At a point overlooking the hut and Friesenberg See, descend with care east down a steep rocky gully system in a series of zigzags over awkward sloping rock ledges. This area is frequently snow covered early in season, with patches of snow remaining throughout the summer.

Thereafter, continue to descend the Uramentenloch rock buttress until the ground naturally eases at the small alpine lake of the **Friesenberg See**, just below the hut. Cross the footbridge and reascend easy slopes to the historic **Friesenberg Haus** (1hr).

## EXCURSION 7.1
*Ascent of Hoeher Riffler (3228m)*

| | |
|---|---|
| **Start** | Friesenberg Haus |
| **Distance** | 2km |
| **Ascent** | 750m |
| **Standard ascent time** | 3hrs |

Those who leave early from the Olperer Hut will find that the Hoeher Riffler, climbed by the southeast ridge, provides an interesting afternoon excursion. The summit has excellent views in all directions, particularly so across the Gefrone Wand Spitze, the Olperer and the peaks of Hintertux.

From the **Friesenberg Haus** proceed north (signpost) for a short distance, then turn northeast up and over rocks and boulders, heading in the direction of an obvious col at the foot of the Hoeher Riffler's south ridge and junction with the line of cliffs that form the Wesendleskar Schneide ridge and the satellite peak of Peterskopfl (2677m) (½hr) (signpost).

From the col at 2628m head northwest, keeping left of the Riffler's south ridge, zigzagging up a well laid-out rocky staircase trail to the first hump or step on the south ridge (1hr).

The route now steepens, zigzagging to and fro across difficult ground over and around large boulders and blocks – be observant and watch out, as the way ahead is not always obvious. A further ½hr leads to a small plateau and the top of the second hump, which so happens to be ideal for a photo stop. Continue along the ridge, crossing patches of snow to exit, where you are confronted by a steep rock buttress; turn this on the right, which is quite exposed. Continue to follow the line of the arête of the buttress to emerge on top of the third hump (1hr).

From hereon the route pitches up and steepens another few degrees to emerge on the ridge overlooking the Spannagelhaus cable-car station. Keep to the bulk of the mountain, as parts of the ridge are very exposed with some sizeable drops. Continue along the ridge, crossing permanent snow cover on the 3000m contour, heading for a low point on the southeast ridge. Scramble up steep rocks to gain the ridge proper. Thereafter follow the obvious ridge line over rocks, with patches of snow, to the summit of **Hoeher Riffler** with its large metal cross (1hr). ▶

This last section offers some excellent mountaineering situations – being very exposed in places and quite airy, with some astonishing drops!

*Approaching the summit of the Hoeher Riffler*

The view from the summit is extensive in all directions – and all four of Austria's highest peaks are visible. The immediate view lies across the void to the Gefrorne Wand Spitze cable-car station. This leads the eye to the near horizon and the triangular wedge and bulk of the Olperer. Further afield to the south and southeast is the Hochfeiler massif, and beyond is the Italian Dolomites. To the east Austria's highest mountain, the Gross Glockner, stands proud, together with the well-defined snowy ridge of the Gross Venediger (the fourth highest peak). To the west are the mountains of the Oetztal and Stubai Alps, with the Schrankogel, Wiesskogel (third highest) and Wild Spitze (second) all clearly visible. Then, lastly, to the north lie the limestone peaks of the Karwendal and the Zug Spitze in neighbouring Germany.

Special attention needs to be exercised in the mid- to upper sections of the climb, both in ascent and descent, as the route is quite steep and very exposed in places, particularly on the summit ridge overlooking the summer ski slopes of the Gefrorne Wand Spitze. While the route has been remarked in recent years, route finding around the mid-section is not always obvious, and this becomes more difficult when it is snow covered.

# EXCURSION 7.2
*Ascent of Peterskopfl (2677m)*

| Start | Friesenberg Haus |
|---|---|
| **Distance** | 1km |
| **Ascent** | 200m |
| **Standard ascent time** | 30–45mins |

This is a first-class short excursion, ideal for a picnic and for those who aspire to be sculptors or stone masons!

From the **Friesenberg Haus**, follow the route description for the ascent of the Hoeher Riffler (see Excursion 7.1) as far as the col below the Riffler's south ridge. At the col, turn right and head south along a vague trail on the craggy cliffs of the Wesendleskar Schneide ridge, then scramble up rocks immediately below the summit.

The summit plateau of **Peterskopfl** is littered by stone cairns of every description, many of which defy the rules of gravity, and are all said to represent those souls lost

*Stone cairns on the Peterskopfl, with the Hochfeiler in the distance*

to the holocaust in the Second World War. There are excellent views across the whole of the Zillertal – the Hochfeiler, Berliner Spitze and the snowy slopes of the Schwarzenstein are all easy to identify and pick out, while those with very sharp eyes will be able to locate the Berliner Hut at the head of the Zemmgrund valley.

# STAGE 8
*Friesenberg Haus to the Gams Hut*

| | |
|---|---|
| **Start** | Friesenberg Haus (2477m) |
| **Finish** | Gams Hut (1916m) |
| **Distance** | 13km |
| **Ascent** | About 1000m (just a lot of up and down) |
| **Standard time** | 10–12hrs |
| **Note** | Official timing for the route between huts is 7–8hrs in either direction. Unless you are very fit these times are woefully inadequate, and it is unlikely that you would cover the distance and terrain involved. More realistic times are 10–12hrs from the Friesenberg Haus and 12hrs from the Gams Hut. Be out of the hut for 06.00 – having breakfast en route will ensure you arrive at the Gams Hut before dark! |

This stage is the sting in the tail at the end of the Zillertal Rucksack Route. It takes you from the highest hut in the Zillertal to the lowest, but don't let that fool you into thinking that the route is all downhill – it isn't! The route traverses up and down roughly on the 2000m contour high above the Zamsergrund valley for its entire length.

While the route is very long, there are excellent views throughout this exploration of the valleys and main Zillertal peaks. The route is superb for wildlife and flowers, being home to the gamsbok mountain antelope, marmot and eagles, plus a countless variety of alpine flowers, particularly alpine rose bushes and Martigon lilies. In mountaineering terms, the route provides a constantly changing panoramic scene – from the ice and rock at Friesenberg Haus to the pretty high alpine pastures at Pitzen and Feldl alms.

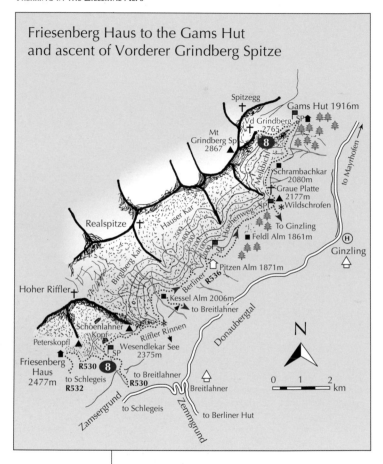

Friesenberg Haus to the Gams Hut and ascent of Vorderer Grindberg Spitze

The route can be split into four distinct sections.

**Friesenberg Haus to Kessel Alm**
From **Friesenberg Haus** Route 530 contours east around and across the ridge coming down from Peterskopfl and affords the last, and perhaps the best, view of the hut before being consigned to memory. Thereafter,

descend broken ground to a signpost pointing the way to the Gams Hut and the descent route to Breitlahner. The route now continues as Route 536, heading north-easterly past a small lake, **Wesendlekar See** (2375m), and ascending slightly over a boulder-strewn slope below the Schoenlahner Kopf. This type of ground is interesting but demands close attention. ▸

Continue as before in a north-easterly direction, then more north under the crags of the **Riffler Rinnen**, eventually giving way in a zigzag descent to a footbridge and the tiny alm at **Kessel Alm** (2006m, 4hrs) (signpost). ▸ This is a first-class place for a rest and a drink, with entertaining views along the Zemmgrund valley and across the void to the Berliner Hut.

### Kessel Alm to Pitzen Alm

Having descended into the open combe that forms the Birglberg Kar, lost height has to be regained by ascending grassy slopes for 100m to reach the 2100m contour. The

Watch out for gamsbok – small alpine antelope – on the lower slopes.

It is the ascent of these slopes in reverse that adds the time when coming from the Gams Hut.

*Crossing boulders of the Riffler Rinnen*

This is roughly the halfway point of the route – those who are not faring too well should perhaps consider descending to Ginzling.

route now crosses two spurs before descending through unpleasant vegetated slopes, which can prove problematic as the path is frequently wet and slippery. Continue through fields to **Pitzen Alm** (1871m), where (provided the Bauer (farmer) or Jager (hunter) is in residence) refreshments may be available (2hrs) (signpost). ◄

## Pitzen Alm to Graue Platte

From the delightful **Pitzen Alm** the track continues northeast along the 1800m contour, passing through the trees of the high alp to emerge at Feldl Alm (1865m). From here the track makes a rising traverse northeast to Graue Platte, first passing through dwarf pine trees followed by boulder fields to the small col that forms the **Graue Platte** (2177m) (2hrs) (signpost). There is excellent scenery hereabouts, particularly the view up the Gunggl valley leading up to the prominent Zsigmondy Spitze. ◄

This point provides a further opportunity to descend to Ginzling should the need arise.

## Graue Platte to the Gams Hut

After reaching the col of the **Graue Platte** the route descends steeply into the broad combe of **Melkbichl**, where many streams congregate (good place for flowers), and crosses more broken ground to reach the tiny alm of **Schrambachkar** at 2080m. From here the route goes northeast then north up and down through boulders, scrub forest, and typical alpine paths before making a zigzag descent off the ridge coming down from the Grindberg Spitze to the **Gams Hut** at 1916m with its bright copper roof (2hrs).

This stage is not as demanding in mountaineering terms as the Edel Hut to the Kasseler Hut connection (ZRR Stage 2) nor as serious as some of the other stages, as the route has a good number of places from which it can be abandoned in favour of descending to the charming village of Ginzling. However, the route's main difficulty is its length, followed by a more subtle problem of route finding, which can be difficult when the trail is overgrown with vegetation and the visibility is poor. The route is therefore unsuitable for novices and should not be undertaken in less than favourable weather.

# EXCURSION 8.1

*Ascent of Vorderer Grindberg Spitze (2765m)*

| | |
|---|---|
| **Start** | Gams Hut |
| **Distance** | 2km |
| **Ascent** | 824m |
| **Standard ascent time** | 3hrs |
| **Note** | Close attention is required when scrambling through and around the massive boulders in the rock garden and the rocks close to the summit. |

An ascent of the Grindberg Spitze is a delightful little climb offering some very good scenery. The mountain dominates the head of the valley above Mayrhofen and comprises three summits, the Vorderer, Mittler and Hinterer, being the fore summit, middle summit and summit beyond. The route described goes only as far as the Vorderer, as the route over the Mittler and Hinterer is a more serious undertaking. The highlight of the route is without doubt the rock garden, which provides some excellent scrambling and some good photo opportunities.

From the **Gams Hut**, retrace your steps along the path of Route 534, heading west to join the junction of the track leading to the Graue Platte (½hr) (signpost for Grindberg Spitze and Friesenberg Haus).

Continue west up easy zigzags, through alpine rose bushes, to join the main ridge proper coming down from the Grindberg. At this point, a crucifix cross is clearly visible across the void on the Spitzegg (2647m, 1hr).

From hereon the route becomes more serious and exposed as the steepness of the ridge increases. The route continues to zigzag through broken ground and a rock garden of house-sized boulders, which provides interesting scrambling requiring four points of contact with the

TREKKING IN THE ZILLERTAL ALPS

*Spectacular scenery amid house-sized boulders in the rock garden*

Look out for gamsbok and marmots – you will hear the marmot's shrill warning whistle breaking the silence.

rock on the more demanding sections. There is excellent scenery hereabouts, particularly in the rough and tumble of the huge boulders. ◄

At approximately 2700m the summit cross on the **Vorderer Grindberg Spitze** becomes clearly visible, making an obvious target for the final pull up to the summit (2½hrs). From the summit the views are extensive, although the mighty snow-capped peaks which have become so familiar en route have now receded to the far horizon, making way for lesser known peaks above Finkenberg and Mayrhofen.

Descend by the same route in reverse, this takes about 1–1½hr giving sufficient time in the afternoon to descent to Ginzling, Finkenberg and Mayrhofen if that is your wish, if not salute your achievement and enjoy your evening in the Gemutlichkeit tradition and charm of the Gams Hut.

From the summit you may be tempted to cross the linking ridge to the Mittler Grindberg. However, the continuation of the route to the Mittler and Hinterer is beyond the scope of this guide, and walkers are advised to stay put. When the interconnecting ridge between the Vorder and Mittler is snow free, the connecting ridge has some good interesting scrambling of Grade II. The route from the Mittler to the Hinterer requires the use of ropes, having a rock climbing grade of IV.

# STAGE 9

*Gams Hut to Mayrhofen*

| | |
|---|---|
| **Start** | Gams Hut (1916m) |
| **Finish** | Mayrhofen (633m) |
| **Distance** | 4km to Ginzling; 3km to Finkenberg |
| **Ascent** | None; all downhill |
| **Standard time** | 3hrs to Ginzling; 2hrs to Finkenberg |

There is a choice of routes to complete the final stage of the Zillertal Rucksack Route, down to either Ginzling or Finkenberg (and by bus to Mayrhofen).

## Gams Hut to Ginzling

From the **Gams Hut** the path descends the Georg Herholz Weg, in a continuation of the east-to-west ridge coming down from the Grindberg Spitze. The track enters a woodland environment with several pleasant alpine glades, and descends in a series of zigzags, some of which are quite steep and can be quite slippery when wet.

Once on the valley floor the quiet of the forest is broken as the path continues through farmland to a bridge over the loud roar of the Zemmbach river. The path along the left bank of the river is avalanche prone and not always open. If it is temporarily closed there will be a 'Gesprutt' sign to indicate this, and walkers should follow the path on and off at the side of the road into **Ginzling**. A lunch stop is highly recommended at the Alte Ginzling Hotel for the best fresh trout in the Zillertal, before continuing by bus (10.10/11.10/14.30/16.10/17.10) to end the tour in **Mayrhofen**.

## Gams Hut to Finkenberg

From the **Gams Hut** descend northeast across the pleasant slopes of the Gamsberg, then more steeply down

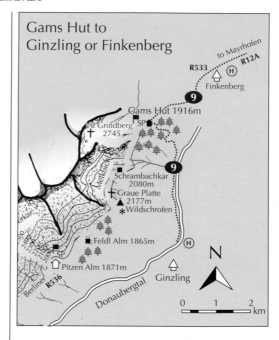

through the forest following the Hermann Hecht Weg (R533) and losing 600m of height. At the foot of the Nesselwand (1305m) the route turns north, descending over alpine pasture to enter the tiny village of **Finkenberg** at its western edge. Here there are signs for Teufelsbrucke, the gravity-defying Devil's Bridge over the Zillerbach, and Route 12A into Mayrhofen.

Those with time on their hands and energy to spare may choose to walk into **Mayrhofen** (about 1hr), while others may wish to dine in Finkenberg at one of the pleasant hotels before finally taking the bus (09.51/10.51/11.51/12.21/13.51/14.51) to Mayrhofen.

# ZILLERTAL SOUTH TYROL TOUR

*On the Schwarzenstein (Stage 7)*

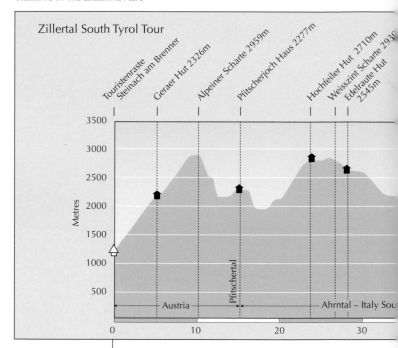

Zillertal South Tyrol Tour

No visit to the Zillertal would be complete without making an excursion to explore the Zillertal peaks of the South Tyrol. The 'South Tyrol' refers to the now Italian South Tyrol, a formerly Austrian province that was annexed to Italy after the First World War. As a result of this annexation, the Deutscher und Osterreichischer Alpenverein lost a total of 72 huts, all forfeited to Italy as war reparations, including the four huts that are visited during this short exploratory tour.

This Zillertal South Tyrol Tour is about 55km long and ascends just over 5000m. You reach it from the approach to the Brenner Pass into Italy at the small town of Steinach am Brenner. From here the post bus runs to the start point of the tour at the farming alm at Touristenraste in the Valsertal valley, where the tour begins with a short

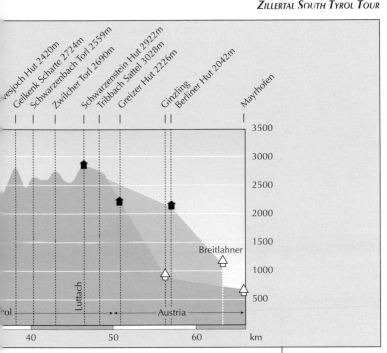

walk to the Geraer Hut. The tour enters the Zillertal and South Tyrol by heading to the privately owned Pfitscherjoch Haus, just above Schlegeis at the head of the Zamsergrund valley and Mayrhofen. This is where trekkers starting from Mayrhofen join the route.

From Pfitscherjoch Haus the tour continues with a visit to the Hochfeiler Hut to climb the Zillertal's highest peak, the Hochfeiler (3510m), and the only peak in the Zillertal over 3500m. Thereafter the Neveser and Stabebeler Hoehenweg are followed to the historic Edelraute and Nevesjoch huts, from where the Grosser Moseler is climbed, with an option to descend the mountain across the border into Austria. The final challenge of this tour is the demanding hut-to-hut route to the EU-protected Schwarzenstein Hut. Then last, the final part of the journey heads across the Schwarzensteinkees or Floitenkees glaciers back into Austria to either the Greizer or Berliner Hut on the ZRR. From there walkers return to Mayrhofen.

Throughout the tour there are constant reminders of past conflicts, notably the impact of both the First and Second World Wars, and the cross-border smuggling and insurgency that were rife during these desperate times of civil strife.

## A BRIEF HISTORY

On crossing the Pfitscherjoch into Italy and the South Tyrol, it's hard to imagine that this whole area almost 100 years ago was a heavily fortified theatre of war.

Italy struggled to remain neutral during the early stages of the First World War, but eventually allied itself with the Entente Alliance (UK, France and Russia) in May 1915, fighting against its former allies Germany and Austria. Four years later, with most of Europe in ruins, Germany had been defeated and the Austrian-Hungarian Empire lay in tatters. The victorious Italians took full control of the South Tyrol from 3 Nov 1918, when the Armistice was proclaimed, and marched north into Austria and Innsbruck to take up occupation of the North Tyrol.

Under the treaty of St Germain (1919), instigated by the Entente Alliance powers, particularly the United States, President Woodrow Wilson ignored a plea for clemency and help by all the mayors of the Sud Tyrol, opting to press ahead with the annexation of the whole of the South Tyrol to Italy, almost as a collective pique of anger as a penalty for starting the war and for war repartitions in general. It was a decision made in haste that Wilson is said to have later deeply regretted. Formal annexation took place on 10 Oct 1920 and affected 150,000 people, a decision that would have a profound effect on the South Tyrol region for the next 50 years.

During the 1920s and 1930s, Austria was a broken and bankrupt country, and this led to much cross-border

*Negotiating difficult ground (Stage 7)*

smuggling and insurgency. Under the open-door pol-icy with Germany in March 1938, Austria became an extended province of Germany, and again the hope was that the South Tyrol would be returned to the Third Reich and German-speaking peoples. That hope was dashed when Germany became allied to Mussolini's fas-cist Italy. In 1939, Mussolini decreed that all the indig-enous German-speaking people of the South Tyrol should become Italianised or leave Italy and the South Tyrol and emigrate to the new lands of the Third Reich and Greater Germany. Of those that did leave, some had little choice, including the Huettenwirtin at the Edelraute Hut. Most went to German-annexed western Poland, where after the war they were persecuted as Nazi sympathisers; similarly, those that stayed in the South Tyrol were persecuted by the Italians.

After the surrender of Italy in 1943, the South Tyrol (including all the huts along its border) was occupied by the German army until the eventual German retreat and surrender of Austria in 1945. By 1948 most of the huts had been returned to the rightful owners, although most were in a ruinous state and those that weren't were occupied by the Italian military.

The South Tyrol political question subsequently raised its head once more, with Austria asking for the return of the South Tyrol. Counter-insurgency across the border and smuggling of goods once again became rife. All the huts along the South Tyrol became garrisoned by the Italian army, and when they did eventually vacate them in the late 1960s and 1970s most huts were in ruins or had been blown up.

In 1972 the South Tyrol was decreed a bilingual semi-autonomous state of Italy, the ties with Austria being strengthened when Austria joined the European Union and the border controls with Italy disappeared, particularly across the Brenner Pass, which went some way to reuniting Austria with its beloved South Tyrol.

Finally, despite all this conflict and the spilt blood of two world wars, the South Tyrol is now the most productive and wealthy state in Italy.

## ALTERNATIVE START FROM SCHLEGEIS

Walkers can start the ZSTT from Mayrhofen and thereby miss out Stages 1 and 2. Take the local bus service from Mayrhofen to Schlegeis (see Introduction, 'The Zillertal Valley and Mayrhofen', for bus times), then follow the route description at ZRR Stage 6a to the Pfitscherjoch Haus.

# STAGE 1

*Touristenraste to the Geraer Hut*

| | |
|---|---|
| **Start** | Touristenraste (1345m) |
| **Finish** | Geraer Hut (2326m) |
| **Distance** | 5km |
| **Ascent** | 800m |
| **Standard time** | 3–4hrs |

What could be better than to start your tour at the hamlet of Touristenraste – full of colour and Tyrolean charm!

From Innsbruck railway station, the Hauptbahnhof, take a regional train to Steinach am Brenner, a small town on the Austrian side of the Brenner Pass (departures at 09.22/10.22/11.22). Should you have to stay overnight in Steinach, the Zur Rose Hotel is recommended (see Appendix B).

From the railway station in Steinach get the local post bus service by the railway station to **Touristenraste** Bergbauernhof farm guest house in the Valsertal valley, a journey just short of 1hr. ▸

Note there is no bus service on Sunday but there is a local taxi service.

From the Touristenraste guest house, continue up the Valsertal valley to the end of the service track road to the **Seilbahn** goods hoist lift for the hut (¾hr) (signpost).

From here, follow the obvious trail northeast on a good path through the forest for a short 2hrs to farm buildings and an alm at **Ochsnerhuette** (2081m), on the grassy slopes of Alpein Alm (2hrs). Once into open landscape the easygoing trail climbs steadily heading southeast and eventually crosses two footbridges and a small gorge of Windschaufelgraben, with a river, not to distant from the hut.

There is a good path all the way to the **Geraer Hut** on long looping zigzags (3–4hrs in total).

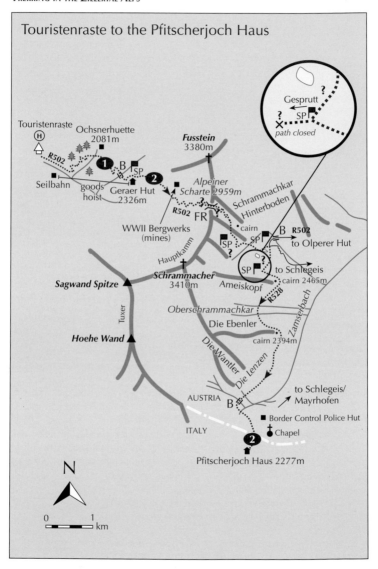

# Touristenraste to the Pfitscherjoch Haus

Touristenraste

Ochsnerhuette
2081m

*Fusstein*
3380m

R502

Seilbahn

goods hoist

Geraer Hut
2326m

B
SP

②

①

*Alpeiner Scharte 2959m*

Schrammachkar

Hinterboden

WWII Bergwerks (mines)

R502

FR

?

cairn

B    R502

to Olperer Hut

SP

SP    ?

SP

to Schlegeis

Hauptkamm

*Schrammacher*
3410m

Ameiskopf

cairn 2465m

*Sagwand Spitze*

R528

*Oberschrammachkar*

Zamselbach

Tuxer

*Die Ebenler*

*Hoehe Wand*

cairn 2394m

*Die Wantler*

*Die Lenzen*

to Schlegeis/
Mayrhofen

AUSTRIA

B

Border Control Police Hut

Chapel

ITALY

②

N

Pfitscherjoch Haus 2277m

0          1
▬▬▬▬ km

Gesprutt

?

SP

?

*path closed*

134

# STAGE 2
## Geraer Hut to Pfitscherjoch Haus

| | |
|---|---|
| **Start** | Geraer Hut (2326m) |
| **Finish** | Pfitscherjoch Haus (2277m) |
| **Distance** | 10km |
| **Ascent** | About 1300m |
| **Standard time** | 6–7hrs |
| **Note** | A landslip obliterated a section of the trail in 2002. The route diversion down into the stone-swept couloir of Hinterboden is not yet well worn and route finding here is very problematic in mist and rain. |

On a fine sunny day this tour is in the top drawer of alpine walks, being challenging and scenically interesting, and having a little Second World War history thrown in for good measure. It crosses one of the few weaknesses in the main Tuxer Hauptkamm ridge.

From the **Geraer Hut** (signpost) follow Route 502 on the Central Alpine Way – if it is a clear day the Alpeiner Scharte will be clearly visible to the east. The path of sorts progresses across broken rocky ground, where after 1hr or so remants of mining activity come into view (1hr). ◄ From here the path becomes steeper and less obvious. Continue as before over open rocky slopes, but now with more slabs and boulders, zigzagging to and fro. Just below the **Alpeiner Scharte** the path steepens considerably (fixed wires in place) to the col (1½–2hrs) (signpost).

The old buildings and steel structures and pylons, now in ruins, were used during the Second World War to mine chrome molyibnium used for making chrome steel.

From the col, descend the very steep rocky slope, first east then southeast over difficult ground of shale and loose rock, until the slope gradually eases at a huge man-made **cairn**. Continue south over open rocky ground, descending gradually for a short kilometre until the path becomes blocked and peters out at a gulley and old glacial moraine (1hr).

Here the track was washed out by a landslide in 2002, forcing the track to be diverted east into the large open corrie of **Schrammachkar** to pick up the trail and hut connection to the Olperer Hut. ◄ Descend northeast over difficult broken ground following the left bank of the stream and attendant moraine, heading for the large open marshy area of Hinterboden, complete with a number of small alpine tarns and ponds. After about 100m of descent, cross the moraine and stream east, heading across open country to pick up the trail of **Route 502** coming from the Olperer Hut. ◄ Thereafter reascend the rocky slope southwest to reconnect with the original path to complete the detour (on this side of the detour is a very large signboard stating that the route ahead is closed and 'Gesprutt') (1hr).

Back on the trail proper, but now on **Route 528**, head southeast on a very good rocky path to a large manmade stone cairn at the foot of the spur on the **Ameiskopf** ridge. Round the foot of the ridge and traverse around the open amphitheatre-type corrie of the **Oberschrammachkar**

This diversion (until the trail is restored) will add at least 1hr to your time as you detour around what was previously 500m of open ground.

The signposts here are not obvious, particularly in mist.

*At Pfitscherjoch, looking towards Austria – with the old border police customs post and chapel*

*Pfitscherjoch Haus*

boulder field, heading for a second large manmade stone cairn 1km away, and crossing two glacial rivers on the way. ▶

Continue as before, southwest, on an excellent rocky path that has been painstakingly laid out and is partly paved in places, traversing the rocky slopes of **Die Ebenler** and **Die Wantler** until the headwaters of the Zamserbach stream and river are reached. Fortunately this noisy raging water is crossed by a footbridge (2hrs).

The track of sorts heads south over open rocky ground, interspersed with streams and marshy ground, to eventually join the broad track coming up the valley from Schlegeis and Mayrhofen. After a short stroll emerge on the border with the South Tyrol at the old border control and customs police hut (the Zollwachhuette). Continue 300m further along the now graded single-track road to reach the **Pfitscherjoch Haus** (1hr).

Excellent views towards Schlegeis and the Zillertal valley.

This is, in the main, a fine-weather route. Crossing the Alpeiner Scharte at just a little short of 3000m means that if it is raining at the Geraer Hut it is definitely sleeting, if not snowing, at the Scharte. The top of the Alpeiner Scharte on both sides of the col is exceedingly steep, and despite the availability of fixed wires it is not a place to be practising snow skills. Thereafter, crossing the numerous streams at Die Lenzen is not without drama, particularly if they are in flood, as these streams are more raging torrent than babbling brook. If you are in a group stay close together for support.

# STAGE 3
*Pfitscherjoch Haus to the Hochfeiler Hut*

| | |
|---|---|
| **Start** | Pfitscherjoch Haus (2277m) |
| **Finish** | Hochfeiler Hut (2710m) |
| **Distance** | 8km |
| **Ascent** | 900m |
| **Standard time** | 6–7hrs |
| **Note** | While there are a number of footbridges en route, they are known at times not to survive the winter. |

This is a particularly fine walk with an excellent variety of alpine scenery. The initial stages are dominated by a chocolate-box scene down the Pfitschertal valley to St Jakob, which is all but lost on entering the forest and woodland area. The mountains reveal themselves once more when the Hochfeiler Hut comes into view. From here on you are in fine alpine territory, with open rocky terrain of spiky pinnacles and some of the finest glaciated and snow-covered peaks in the Zillertal.

From the **Pfitscherjoch Haus**, head off south along the hut's service road. After about 100m some old army buildings are passed, which were occupied by the Austrians prior to the First World War, then the Italian military until the early 1960s. Continue down the road to a signpost indicating the first of several shortcuts across the service road. Head off southwest across the easy-going open grassy slopes of the **Via Alpina** trail, where the observant will be able to pick out old army trench systems, albeit overgrown, from an era fortunately long past. The path descends first gradually over open ground then, after about 1km, more steeply when it enters woodland to join the service road once more. The service road turns southeast, and after a further 1km comes to a car

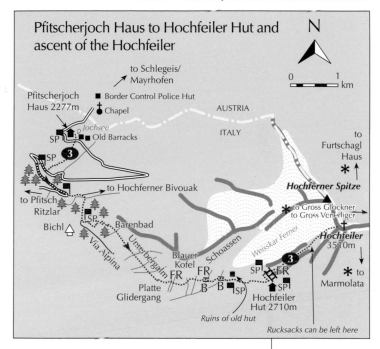

Pfitscherjoch Haus to Hochfeiler Hut and ascent of the Hochfeiler

N

to Schlegeis/ Mayrhofen

Pfitscherjoch Haus 2277m
■ Border Control Police Hut
✝ Chapel

AUSTRIA

0    1 km

*Jochsee*
SP
■ Old Barracks

ITALY

to Furtschagl Haus

✳ ↑

SP **3**

to Hochferner Bivouak

*Hochferner Spitze*

to Pfitsch Ritzlar
SP

✳ to Gross Glockner
to Gross Venediger →

Bichl △
*Barenbad*

*Via Alpina*
*Unterbergalm*

*Schoassen*

*Weisskar Ferner*

✳ ↑ *Hochfeiler* 3510m

Blauer Kofel

FR   FR
B   B   SP
Platte Glidergang

SP   FR
SP
Hochfeiler Hut 2710m

**3**

✳ to Marmolata

*Ruins of old hut*

*Rucksacks can be left here*

park and picnic area noted as **Ritzlar** (1750m, 1½hrs) (signpost). ▶

Head off south following a good path through the quiet of the forest to a group of farm-type woodland buildings at **Bichl** (signpost). The path now pitches up a few degrees and starts to climb, zigzagging up vegetated slopes east and gradually emerging onto more open ground on the 2000m contour at **Barenbad** (1hr).

The track, now more of a rocky path than vegetated trail, continues to climb steadily for another hour across the open slopes of the Unterbergalm, coming to a natural conclusion at **Platte Glidergang**. From here, on rounding the rocky buttress **Blauer Kofel**, the Hochfeiler Hut comes into view – some 500m higher and still over 2km away (1–1½hrs). ▶

The signpost declares that the Hochfeiler Hut is some 3hrs 10mins distant, but in reality it is 4hrs.

Good place for a break, with fine views towards the glaciated peaks and Hoher Weisszint.

*Crossing boulder slopes below Schoassen, with the Hochfeiler Hut circled*

The character of the route now becomes more mountainous. Climb the rocky slopes ahead and traverse east, under the crags of **Schoassen**. Cross a number of gullies with fixed wires in place before descending towards the foot of the terminal moraine of the **Weisskar Ferner** glacier, where many streams congregate. Cross over the streams, making use of the footbridges, to the start of the zigzags leading to the hut (signpost). The left-hand track leads to the site of the original Wiener Hut that was blown up in 1962 by the Italian army as a deterrent to South Tyrolean would-be insurgents and smugglers. However, the main track is the one to the right that climbs the gravel path more gradually to the very robust **Hochfeiler Hut** (2½–3hrs).

Those interested in alpine history should spend some time searching out the location of the old **Wiener Hut**. The Victorian artist ET Compton painted a scene of the hut in 1900, and it might be interesting to ponder where he pitched his canvas and easel. The picture was gifted to the Austrian Alpine Club in 1966 and now hangs proudly in the Alpenvereins Museum in Innsbruck.

This is a fine-weather route, as rain would be particularly unpleasant in the woodland and forest areas. The only other difficulties involve rounding the crags above Platte Glidergang and crossing the boulder ground at Weisskar.

# EXCURSION 3.1
## Ascent of the Hochfeiler (3510m)

| | |
|---|---|
| **Start** | Hochfeiler Hut |
| **Distance** | 2km |
| **Ascent** | 800m |
| **Grade** | F+ |
| **Standard ascent time** | 3hrs |
| **Note** | During dubious weather the route is best avoided, as the ridge and snow arête leading to the summit attract fierce strong winds that will bowl you over. |

A justifiably popular climb on the Zillertal's highest peak – the Hochfeiler is the only peak in the Zillertal over 3500m. The route is characterised by excellent scrambling along the southwest ridge and finishes with an airy snow arête climb to the summit. The route (minus any serious glacial obstacles) is very straightforward, with only the last 500m of height requiring modest alpine skills.

From the **Hochfeiler Hut** (signpost) head north, climbing a buttress aided with wire ropes, metal staples and gangway planks, to the junction of the alternative path coming up from the site of the old Wiener Hut (½hr) (signpost).

Turn right, northeast, and follow the well-defined ridge, climbing steadily over rock, slabs and boulders. At point 3119m the route opens up, revealing the profile of the final

*Summit view along the frontier ridge looking towards the Grosser Moseler (left) and Gross Venediger on the far horizon*

The first ascent was made in 1865 by P Grohmann, P Fuchs and G Samer.

ridge and snow arête leading to the summit of the Hochfeiler – with its attendant cross looking particularly fine.

Continue to climb over rocks, patches of snow and general broken ground, heading for an obvious dip and col on the ridge (2hrs). This is a very good place to stop and tackle up with rope, ice axe and crampons. The scenery is exceptional, as the panorama now includes the Hochfeiler's neighbouring peaks of Hochferner Spitze and Hoher Weisszint.

Continue now in the obvious direction of the ridge and summit beyond. Climb and scramble along the ridge, keeping north on the least exposed side until the rocks meet the snow. From here, climb the short snow arête to the summit of **Hochfeiler** and large metal cross (½hr). ◀

The views from the summit are extensive – sharp eyes will be able to locate the Furtschagl Haus, just 3km away and 1200m lower to the north. If you take care and walk along the ridge beyond the summit the views are exceptional, with everything draped in snow, particularly down the Hochfeiler's north face and across the void to the Grosser Moseler and Schwarzenstein. Beyond, all the major peaks are easy to pick out, such as Olperer, Oetztal Wild Spitze, Gross Glockner and the Dolomites, with the Marmolata to the south.

# STAGE 4

*Hochfeiler Hut to the Edelraute Hut*

| | |
|---|---|
| **Start** | Hochfeiler Hut (2710m) |
| **Finish** | Edelraute Hut (2545m) |
| **Distance** | 4km |
| **Ascent** | 250m |
| **Standard time** | 3hrs |
| **Note** | The sign outside the Hochfeiler Hut states that the Edelraute Hut is a mere 1½hrs away – but in this time you will get only as far Untere Weisszint Scharte. |

This is a very pleasant walk to one of the most traditional huts in the South Tyrol. Much of the day's route – and the whole of the previous day's climb on the Hochfeiler – can be seen from the terrace of the Hochfeiler Hut.

From the **Hochfeiler Hut**, head off east up the rocky boulder slopes that overlook the **Glider Ferner glacier** and gradually descend tottering blocks to the glacier at a little over the 2800m contour (¾hr) (signpost). Get onto the glacier – there is no need to tackle up unless it is snow covered, as the glacier is fairly flat and covered in grit, negating the need for crampons. Cross the glacier south for 500m, heading for a large rock buttress. ▶ Climb the buttress, making use of the staples, ladder rungs and fixed wires; there are some stiff pull-ups until the ground gradually eases.

Anyone who cannot reach the first of the ladder rungs should descend the side of the buttress and round its base to a snow gully that can be climbed just as easily as the aid-assisted route. From the top of the buttress the route traverses more open ground and patches of snow and rocks (again fixed wires in places) to finally emerge on the little col of **Untere Weisszint Scharte** (2930m,

Excellent views towards the Hochfeiler and Hoher Weisszint.

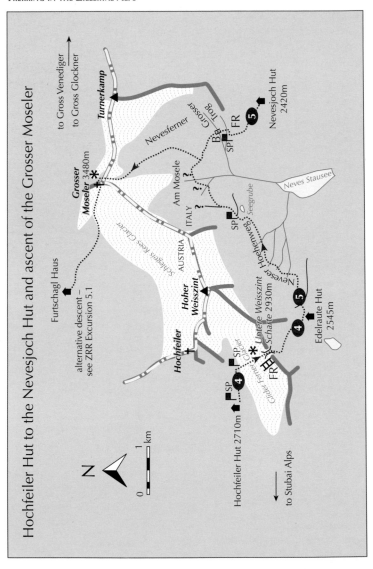

Hochfeiler Hut to the Nevesjoch Hut and ascent of the Grosser Moseler

2hrs) (signpost). From the col the Edelraute Hut is clearly visible.

*Above the Glider Ferner glacier, with Hochfeiler on the far left*

Vews from the little col are particularly interesting as the land is placed in a sort of clear geographic context. Looking west are the peaks of the Stubai Alps, and (should you have binoculars with you) it should be possible to locate the Becher Haus perched on its tiny rocky knoll just to the left of the Wilder Freiger. Looking east towards the hut, the jagged peaks of the Dolomites break the horizon like a row of saw teeth. The snowy mantel of the Marmolata stands clear, and the long plateau of Sieser Alm is very easy to locate, as are individual massifs of Rosengarten and Zwolferkofel. ▶

From the Scharte descend southeasterly through a trail of large boulders (some equipped with fixed wires on the exposed sections) until the path gradually eases into a fine rocky paved trail to the very pleasant **Edelraute Hut**, perhaps better known on this side of the border by its Italian name, Rifugio Ponte di Ghiaccio, or as the Eisbruggjoch, named after the broad saddle on which it sits.

This little col picks up an excellent mobile telephone signal – making even international telephone calls possible!

Getting down the moraine onto the glacier needs to be undertaken carefully, as it is just loose rubble and not very stable underfoot. Getting off the glacier and climbing the rock buttress with the ladder rungs is fine if you can reach them; otherwise you may have to ask your companion for a foot-up. This type of scenario will only get more common as glaciers recede and aids gets further out of reach.

## STAGE 5
*Edelraute Hut to the Nevesjoch Hut*

| | |
|---|---|
| **Start** | Edelraute Hut (2545m) |
| **Finish** | Nevesjoch Hut (2420m) |
| **Distance** | 7km |
| **Ascent** | About 200m |
| **Standard time** | 3hrs with an intact footbridge; otherwise 5hrs |
| **Note** | Normally the ravine is bridged; if it has been washed away proceed with utmost care. |

This is a very pleasant route with some very good alpine walking, particularly the early and latter parts of the journey over painstakingly laid-out paved rocky paths. The scenery is good, but not exceptional, as the high peaks are very much guarded. However, the real challenge of the day is in crossing the ravine midway between huts – ask the Edelraute Hut guardian for advice on conditions before you set out.

On leaving behind the very pleasant **Edelraute Hut**, the Nevesjoch Hut is clearly seen across the valley to the east some 6km away as the crow flies, although the journey by foot is a little longer. Head off northeast along the Neveser Hoehenweg on an excellent paved rocky track of delightful alpine walking. ◄ Continue following the

Good retrospective views back to the Edelraute Hut.

*A novel signpost points the way at the Am Mosele*

rocky trail, with the Nevesjoch Hut in clear view ahead, and after 1hr come to a sign of sorts, with various directions painted on a large boulder at **Seegrube** that points the way down the valley (1hr).

Round the corner of the rocky rib and climb gradually up to the 2500m contour, and after another short distance come to a vague track heading off more north.

*Nevesjoch Hut on the*
*Nevesjoch pass*

Get advice from the
guardian at Edelraute
before setting out.

The main hut-to-hut connecting route is the obvious trail ahead, and if it is clear and not barred with a pile of rocks (indicating 'Gesprutt') then continue as before. If the trail ahead is 'Gesprutt', then take your chances and follow the main trail or, alternatively, follow the vague trail heading off left to the north and cross open ground to pick up the trail beyond, but note this traverse is also problematic. ◄

For those following the main path, continue as before and after a short hour come to the head of some zigzags that descend to a washed-out ravine complete with waterfall and a menacing noisy river. Cross this 50m-wide gap by whatever means, then continue over straightforward rocky ground for a short distance. Once more the trail disappears at the edge of another collapsed moraine that has also been washed out, albeit not as seriously as the previous one. Descend the moraine of loose rocks and boulders glued together with mud and grit and reascend the opposite awkward slope of shale and rubble to get back on the path proper and the open level ground of the **Am Mosele** glacial basin. This massive stone-swept amphitheatre of a corrie was left by retreating glaciers and is marked by a large stone cairn. Round the basin to a junction of paths that points the way to the Grosser Moseler (1hr) (signpost). (See Excursion 5.1.)

From here continue over open rocky ground. At its lowest point a simple tree-trunk footbridge is crossed at **Grosser Trog**, where there is another large stone cairn and elaborate signpost pointing out the direction of climbs up Turnerkamp and the Grosser Moseler.

The route continues on much more easygoing terrain, following an excellent paved path with fixed wires on the more exposed sections. On rounding a corner the Edelraute Hut comes back into view as the path descends to the **Nevesjoch Hut**, named after the col on which it sits (1hr).

The crossing of the ravine between the two huts can turn what should be a very pleasant walk of a few hours into something far more serious. Normally this ravine is bridged; unfortunately the bridge often gets washed away in the winter, leaving this section of ground extremely difficult to cross. If the footbridge is in place there is little to hinder the journey; however, if the bridge has gone, you will be seriously challenged, and crossing the ravine will cost you at least 1hr, no matter what route you take.

If there is a bridge, the route ahead should be obvious, but if not retrace your steps to the top of the zigzags and head north over open rocky ground. After 150m of uphill, turn east and make your own way by Hobson's Choice to cross the glacial meltwaters higher up. Once across the stream, more waterfall than babbling brook, it is a similar story in descent – by scrambling down the left bank of the cascading river to pick up the path once more. In the absence of a bridge your alternative is to descend the top edge overlooking the right bank of the ravine for around 100m until it is possible to descend into the gully, cross the river and reascend the moraine-type slope on the opposite bank.

If on leaving the Edelraute Hut the guardian advises the route as 'Gesprutt', then take the vague path as mentioned just beyond Seegrube.

# EXCURSION 5.1

*Ascent of the Grosser Moseler (3480m)*

| | |
|---|---|
| **Start** | Nevesjoch Hut |
| **Distance** | 5.5km |
| **Ascent** | 1100m |
| **Grade** | F+ |
| **Standard ascent time** | 4hrs |
| **Note** | In the last 400m of the summit the terrain is very steep and very exposed when moving together over difficult broken round. This is not a route to undertake in less than ideal weather. |

This popular route on the Zillertal's second highest peak is distinctly different from the route from the north (ZRR Excursion 5.1). Here, from the south, the route is much more straightforward, putting the mountain within the grasp of the most modest of mountaineers. The view from the summit is exceptional.

From the **Nevesjoch Hut**, begin to retrace the route to the Edelraute Hut (Stage 5), heading northwest along the Neveser Hoehenweg. Follow the excellent path first to **Grosser Trog**, marked with the huge stone cairn and novel signpost that indicates the route to the mountain, then continue onwards across open ground to the tree-trunk footbridge, followed by an easy walk over open ground and the lower slopes of the **Am Mosele** boulder field 1¼hrs (signpost).

From here turn and head north over open rocky ground comprised mostly of glacial debris. The route climbs the ridge immediately ahead in a gradual fashion for 1km, when the ridge ramps up steeply a few more degrees and becomes more obstructive. Climb through the

*On the summit – only seven people made it to the top that day!*

rock barrier (fixed ropes in place) until the ground gradually eases on the 3000m contour. With the summit cross in clear view, climb the rocky rib, scrambling here and there over rocks and patches of snow, then veer more northwest heading for an obvious small gap in the Mosele's east ridge. Climb the steepening slope, now more snow than rock, to its obvious conclusion, where on arrival you will simply say 'Wow!', as the scenery is absolutely stunning, with a whole mountain landscape of snow and white drapery, together with wall-to wall-mountains.

*On the Schlegeiskees glacier*

From hereon scramble cautiously along the east ridge for the last 100m of vertical height, very exposed in places, amid alpine scenery at its best. Finally reach **Grosser Moseler's** summit cross, together with a cross-path as your track joins with the route from the north and from Furtschagl Haus.

From the summit the views are exceptional. But it is the view to the north that will hold your attention and gaze, particularly along the east (right) towards Turnerkamp (no easy routes on this mountain); then about-turn to the southwest to the magnificent ice wall and jumbled maze of crevasses on the Hochfeiler and Hochferner. To the northwest, those with sharp eyes will quickly locate the Furtschagl Haus and, beyond, the Schlegeis reservoir, with the Olperer and Shneegupf snow arête. To the south lies the fertile South Tyrol, with the Riesenferner Group, and beyond the unique Dolomites, whose jagged peaks break the horizon like a row of teeth on a saw. Simply stunning. Enjoy!

In descent, either reverse the entire route back to the **Nevesjoch Hut**, but take additional care when descending the first 200m of vertical height when the ground gets easier. Alternatively, descend the mountain to the **Furtschagl Haus** by reversing the route description given when climbing the mountain from the north (see ZRR Excursion 5.1).

# STAGE 6

*Nevesjoch Hut to the Schwarzenstein Hut*

| | |
|---|---|
| **Start** | Nevesjoch Hut (2420m) |
| **Finish** | Schwarzenstein Hut (2922m) |
| **Distance** | 11km |
| **Ascent** | About 1350m ascent and 1060m descent |
| **Standard time** | 8–10 hrs |
| **Note** | Be on your way early, but before setting out reserve a bed with the guardian at the Schwarzenstein Hut. (You don't want to walk for 10hrs only to find that there are no beds.) Also ask the guardian at the Nevesjoch Hut to telephone the Schwarzenstein Hut in the evening to make sure that you have arrived safely. |

This is a very long-distance alpine walk, and one that is not to be underestimated. The route traverses up and down roughly on the 2500m contour high above the Ahrntal valley, rounds three huge mountain corrie amphitheatres and crosses three passes. In mountaineering terms, since the route is almost entirely on rock and traverses a great deal of difficult broken ground, it is rated at the top end of alpine walking, with a constant demand on basic mountain skills from start to finish. If blessed by good weather and blue skies there is excellent scenery throughout.

From the **Nevesjoch Hut** the way ahead is barred by a great wall of mountains that will have to be negotiated. Head off east, along the Stabeler Hoehenweg, on Route 24A, with easy walking following a good path. After a short kilometre a signpost of sorts is reached, with route directions being painted on a large boulder, and

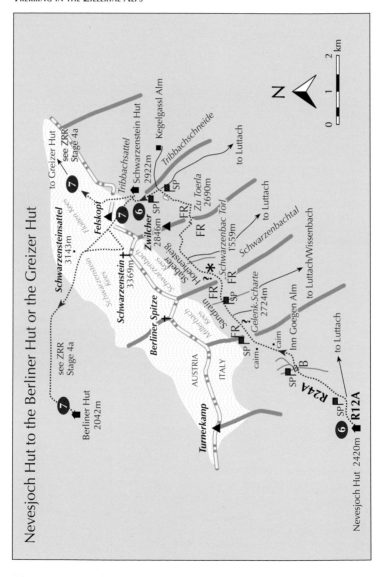

Nevesjoch Hut to the Berliner Hut or the Greizer Hut

to Greizer Hut
see ZRR
Stage 4a

**7**

**7**   Schwarzenstein Hut 2922m
Tribbachsattel

Kegelgassl Alm

Tribbachschneide

to Luttach

**6**   Zwilcher 2846m   SP

Felskopf

Schwarzensteinsattel

Schwarzenstein 3143m

Rollen Kees

SP

FR   Zu Toerla 2690m

to Luttach

FR

Höchriststeig

Schwarzenstein 3369m

Schwarzwenstein Kees

Schwarzenbach

Stabeler   FR

Schwarzenbac Törl 1559m

Schwarzenbachtal   to Luttach

see ZRR
Stage 4a

**7**

Berliner Spitze

Berliner Hut 2042m

Milfbach

Schlegeis Kees

Sandhain

FR   ?

FR   FR

*

Gelenk-Scharte 2724m

SP

to Luttach/Wissenbach

AUSTRIA

ITALY

cairm •

SP   cairm

Inn Goegen Alm

cairn

to Luttach

Turnerkamp

B

**R24A**

SP

**6**   **R12A**

Nevesjoch Hut 2420m

to Luttach

N

0   1   2 km

*Approaching Zu Toerla over difficult ground with boulders everywhere*

a junction with the path coming up the valley from the small village of Luttach. Here the route turns northeast, heading into the upper alp and reaching the marshy grazing meadows of **Inn Goegen Alm**. The route continues to a footbridge and signpost (1hr).

Cross the footbridge and ascend the slopes ahead (northeast), climbing through an obvious rock buttress, with the Scharte col easy to see to the left. As the route levels out head through, over and around various boulder fields, with the usual meandering false trails. The route is part-marked in places with large purpose-built stone cairns and eventually emerges on the first of the three passes to be crossed, the **Gelenk Sharte** (2724m, 2hrs) (signpost). ▶

Fine rugged mountain scenery.

From the col, descend northeast down steep, difficult, ankle-twisting rocky slopes with huge boulders until the ground gradually eases below the peaks of the Berliner Spitze to the north and vast boulder slopes of the Sandrain on the 2460m contour, created from the retreating Mitterbachkees glacier. There is a signpost here indicating the route down the valley to Wiessenbach. Continue to round the head of the couloir and corrie, ascending steep rocky slopes over difficult broken ground (fixed wires here and there) to the second of the three passes, the **Schawarzenbach Torl** (2559m, 2hrs). ◄

The name means 'black gate'.

From the Torl, the terrain dictates how and where you will descend, giving you no choice but to descend the steep gully ahead that is near vertical in places. Descend the gully cautiously, making use of the substantial fixed ropes, until the ground gradually eases. At the base of the Torl, continue northeast on the Stabeler Hoehensteig and Route 24A. Note the change of name from 'Hoehenweg' to 'Hoehensteig', indicating a change from a 'high-level way' to a 'high-level climb' – based on the nature of the ground, it is perhaps a better name. The trail continues over wearisome rocky broken ground that has now become a familiar characteristic of this route. Midway the track is broken with a vague track coming up from the south and Luttach (signpost).

Ahead is the third and highest of the passes to be crossed, the **Zwilcher Torl** (2690m). Continue as before to round the head of the corrie and couloir, climbing gradually then much more steeply on a tight zigzagging rocky trail (fixed wires) to the very enclosed Torl cum gateway, complete with park-bench-type seat and signpost (2hrs). ◄

Excellent views towards the Schwarzenstein, where sharp eyes will be able to locate the hut.

Unfortunately much height has now to be lost. Oh, to be an Adler (eagle) and cross this great open void in a matter of minutes. From the Torl descend the steep rocky slopes of **Zu Toerla** until the ground gradually eases on the 2500m contour. Continue northeast over what is now easy ground, rounding the now familiar corrie-type scenery past a small glacial pond and eventually linking

up with the path coming up from the valley and Luttach (2hrs) (signpost).

Having lost so much height in the descent from the Zwilcher Torl, the sting in the tail is now staring into our face – with the hut perched many metres above our heads! The route turns north, and after a few hundred metres a signpost is reached at Ofenleit that indicates the way to the Schwarzenstein Hut and across the Tribbachschneide ridge to Kegelgassl Alm. Keep left (north) and continue to climb the steepening rocky slopes. After another short distance a second signpost is reached that indicates the Klettersteige and climbing path to the hut. Unless you are blessed with an abundance of energy, it is probably best to stay with the voie normal.

Continue as before, plodding through a glacial basin of huge boulders left by the retreating glacier until it is possible to ascend a large patch of permanent snow. Climb this to its head and make an awkward exit onto the rocks on the right, from where there is a vague trail of

*The magnificent Schwarzenstein Hut*

*Negotiating steep ground and fixed ropes at the Schwarzenstein Toerl*

sorts. Get onto the rocks and traverse the slope in a series of rocky ramps aided by fixed ropes and ladder-type staples until the ridge runs out of mountain and the famous **Schwarzenstein Hut** is eventually reached (2hrs).

Most of the route involves crossing numerous boulder fields; some are typical mountain terrain, while others are high risk – ankle-twisting, leg-snapping terrain scattered with enomous boulders. In addition, the route is very remote and you are unlikely to meet other walkers. The weather is also a major concern, since there is nowhere on the entire route to shelter should you need to. With these two issues, you need to be very confident of your fitness and the weather.

# STAGE 7

*Schwarzenstein Hut to the Berliner Hut or the Greizer Hut*

| | |
|---|---|
| **Start** | Schwarzenstein Hut (2922m) |
| **Finish** | Berliner Hut (2042m) or Greizer Hut (2226m) |
| **Distance** | Berliner Hut 8km; Greizer Hut 4km |
| **Ascent** | Berliner Hut 315m; Greizer Hut 110m |
| **Standard time** | Berliner Hut 6hrs; Greizer Hut 3–4hrs |
| **Note** | If there is poor weather at the Schwarzenstein Hut, making any of the glacier crossings (below) dangerous, then the only safe option is to descend into the Ahrntal valley to Luttach. Get the local bus service to Brunneck, then the regional train service to Brixen, then Sterzing and the Brenner, and across the Austro-Italian border to Innsbruck – a rather tedious but safe journey that will take the whole day. |

A choice of routes back to Austria presents itself, both of which are of equal merit. Descend to the Berliner Hut or the Greizer Hut, and from either you can continue with the ZRR tour or descend to Mayrhofen.

Anyone who made the effort to undertake Stage 4 of the ZRR traversing the Schwarzenstein from the Greizer Hut to the Berliner Hut will have come full circle. Those who opted for the normal route between the Greizer Hut and the Berliner Hut will now have the option to climb the Schwarzenstein that was missed on the first opportunity. What choices indeed!

*On the Schwarzenstein*

### To the Greizer Hut

The descent to the Greizer Hut via the Floitenkees glacier is recommended. This is not a difficult journey, but it is a very good exercise in glacier travel and route finding skills. See ZRR Stage 4a, but reverse the route across the Tribbachsattel (3028m) and the descent across the complex Floitenkees glacier.

### To the Berliner Hut

The recommendation is to follow ZRR Stage 4a from the Schwarzenstein Hut across the Schwarzensteinsattel (3143m) to the Berliner Hut, which includes the option to climb the Schwarzenstein (3369m).

### GETTING TO MAYRHOFEN

If you are not going on to join the Zillertal Rucksack Route, it is a walk of 9km from the Greizer Hut (to Ginzling) and 7km from the Berliner Hut (to Breitlahner) to pick up a local bus back to Mayrhofen. Each walk takes about 3–4hrs and the routes are described and bus times given in the Hut Directory under the entries for each hut ('Day walk from Mayrhofen').

# HUT DIRECTORY

*The Berliner Hut*

# ZILLERTAL MOUNTAIN HUTS

More information is available from the *Alpenvereins Hut Directory Volume 1: Ostalpen*, (previously known as the 'Green book'), published by Rother of Munich, and from tourist offices and the huts themselves.

As more of the Zillertal huts develop websites and email addresses, walkers can easily make reservations online and check for up-to-date information on the huts by visiting

- www.aacuk.org.uk
- www.alpenverein.at
- www.bergsteigen.at/de (click on 'Hutten')
- www.berlinerhoehenweg.at

## ABBREVIATIONS

| B | Bedrooms |
|---|---|
| M | Matratzenlager – dormitory-style accommodation |
| N | Notlager – the winter room or other available space more commonly known as 'sleeping with the furniture' |

## DAY WALKS FROM MAYRHOFEN

All the huts described below, apart from those in the South Tyrol of Italy, connect with the main Zillertal valley and the resort town of Mayrhofen. This means that visitors based in Mayrhofen who want a mountain experience can access all the huts as day walks, starting and finishing at the railway/bus station in Mayrhofen (see individual hut listings for details).

## BERLINER HUT (2042M)

| Owner | DAV Sektion Berlin |
|---|---|
| Location | At the head of the Zemmgrund valley |
| Open | Early June to early October |

| Facilities | 76B/89M/17N Excellent restaurant and toilet facilities, complete with showers and hot water. Everything you would expect from the biggest hut in the Zillertal. |
|---|---|
| Connections | From Mayrhofen, post bus to Breithlahner 09.15/10.15/11.40. Greizer Hut 6–8hrs, Furtschagl Haus 6–7hrs, Breithlahner 3hrs |
| Address | Berliner Huette, Robert and Kirstin Schoeneborn, A-5761 Maria Alm, A-6295 Ginzling, Zillertal |
| Telephone | (0043) 05286 5223 |
| Mobile | (0043) 0676 7051473 |
| Email | berlinerhuette@aon.at |
| Website | www.berlinerhuette.at |

On 28 July 1879 the Berliner Hut had the distinction of being the first hut to be opened in the Zillertal; the hut was subsequently enlarged in 1885. With its ever-increasing popularity, by 1890 the hut was becoming much too small, and an entirely new hut was built in 1892, which in turn was extended in 1911 to its present status.

The current Berliner Hut is a magnificent five-storey building more akin to a mountain lodge fit for royalty than a hut for would-be alpinists! The hut reflects the great wealth and pride of the German Alpine Club at the turn of the 20th century. As a credit to its original architect, and despite increased use over the years, the hut has remained virtually in tact and unchanged except for the addition of modern plumbing and electricity. Indeed such is the hut's importance that it is protected by the European Union as a building of historical significance. The reception hall has a very grand timber staircase complete with decorative timber chandelier, which would have been adorned in the days before electricity with oil lamps. Adjacent walls are graced with important dignitaries, long-deceased Huettenwirts and DAV Presidents. The hut's lofty corridors of creaking timbers are individually styled, reflecting its visitors' various ranks and social status. The timber panelling is from an era long past when the hut was used by the Austrian royal family and the military and political elite as much as a hunting lodge as a base for alpine excursions.

The centrepiece of the hut remains the large and substantial dining room, which in years long ago would have doubled as a ballroom and boomed to the sounds of Strauss and brass bands amid much beer drinking and revelry! Naturally the ladies, exhausted, would have retired to the sanctuary of the adjacent and very private 'ladies room'.

More recently, the hut was used as a base to train the elite forces of the German army during the Second World War. A small memorial below the hut commemorates those DAV Sektion Berlin members, civilian and military, that perished during the conflict.

## Day walk from Mayrhofen

**Post bus to Breithlahner**
**Outward**   09.15/10.15
**Return**    14.15/16.15/17.15

From Breithlahner Bergbauernhof hotel (signpost) follow directions for Route 523. The route follows a graded single-track service road-cum-track that leads initially through the Zemmgrund valley with very pleasant easy alpine walking that embraces forest, various farms and high pasture to end after 2hrs at the Alpenrose Gasthof. There is excellent pastoral scenery hereabouts, but it is still a little too low to see the surrounding peaks.

The graded track ends here and continues as a mountain trail. The path steepens and climbs through diminishing woodland, zigzagging here and there. The rocky trail eventually passes the memorial to DAV Sektion Berlin members who perished during the Second World War, located some 10mins below the hut (3hrs to the hut).

## EDELRAUTE HUT (2545M)

| | |
|---|---|
| **Owner** | CAI Sektion Brixen |
| **Location** | On the broad saddle of Eisbruggjoch |
| **Open** | Mid-June to early October |
| **Facilities** | 50B/40M/10N Good restaurant facilities, with minimal toilet facilities that are cramped when the hut is full. |
| **Connections** | Post bus to/from Lappach and Neves Stausee reservoir 3hrs. Hochfeiler Hut 6hrs, Nevesjoch Hut 4–5hrs |
| **Excursions** | Hochfeiler (3510m) 6hrs, Hoher Weisszint (3371m) 6hrs |
| **Address** | Herr Anton Weissteiner, Edelraute Huette, Ortnerweg 2, I-39042 Brixen, Italy |
| **Telephone** | (0039) 0474 653 230 |
| **Email** | info@edelrautehuette.it |
| **Website** | www.edelrautehuette.it |
| **Note** | Also known as Rifugio Ponte di Ghiaccio and Eisbruggjoch Hut |

This splendid little hut reflects everything that one could wish for when staying at a mountain hut – it is warm, friendly and welcoming in the Gemutlichkeit tradition. It was built in 1908 by the Vienna Mountaineering Club, who named the hut after a flower and a district of Vienna. Ownership of the hut passed to the Alpenverein in 1910, and the hut was renamed in 1914 as the Eisbruggjoch, although there is not the slightest amount of ice anywhere near the hut. During the First World War the hut was closed before being forfeited to Italy in 1919. Having been transferred to the CAI the hut managed to reopen in 1925, being renamed Rifugio Ponte di Ghiaccio.

During the 1920s smuggling in the area was rife, and became so severe that the Italian authorities issued a warning in 1927 – 20–30 years in jail for those caught trafficking wine, schnapps, cigarettes, gold or money. It was at this time that the Italian military started to occupy the huts along the South Tyrol border.

A period of peace and quiet followed until the war cries of Nazi Germany and Fascist Italy began to stir trouble once more in the South Tyrol. In 1939 the Italian dictator Mussolini declared that all German-speaking Sud Tyrolese should leave Italy for good unless they embraced the Italian language and way of life. As a result many Sud Tyrolese folk were forcibly evicted from their homes, including the then female Huettenwirtin, Magdelena, and her daughter Paula and son Sepp. A photograph in the dining room shows the family at Brixen railway station leaving for Germany to an unknown fate and the eventual Second World War.

Situated on the broad saddle of Eisbruggjoch, the hut occupies a wonderful position with excellent views over the Eisbrugg See alpine tarn to the southwest and the peaks of the Hoher Weisszint to the north. The Nevesjoch Hut can clearly be seen across the valley to the east perched on a similar broad saddle of the Nevesjoch, some 3–5hrs distant.

During the Second World War the hut was closed, being occupied by the Italian military who plundered and trashed the hut. Towards the end of the war the hut was strafed several times by the advancing British and American airforce, which left what remained of the hut in ruins. Reconstruction of the hut commenced 1949–51, mostly by the Italian military as recompense for the damage they had caused.

In 1964 the South Tyrol question was again on the political agenda, which resulted in the Italian military once more occupying the hut – and all huts on the border. The army eventually vacated in 1972, and the hut was reopened in 1976. The winter room and external Matratzenlager were rebuilt and opened in 1980, and the hut was reroofed in 1985 after being badly damaged during a storm. The little bell tower on the Matratzenlager roof was added to mark the hut's centenary.

## FRIESENBERG HAUS (2477M)

| | |
|---|---|
| **Owner** | DAV Sektion Berlin |
| **Location** | On the southern flank of the Hoeher Riffler |
| **Open** | Mid-June to end of September |
| **Facilities** | 13B/33M Good restaurant and toilet facilities. Rooms are very tasteful and furnished in the style of old Austria. Debit card payment facility. |
| **Connections** | Mayrhofen via Breitlahner and Ginzling (bus from Mayrhofen 09.15/10.15/11.40; bus from Schlegeis 10.20/12.00/13.55/ 15.55/16.55/17.55). Olperer Hut 3hrs, Gams Hut 10–12hrs, Schlegeis 2hrs |
| **Address** | Herr Hubert Fritzenwallner, Friesenberg Haus, Grubl Strasse 13, A-5621 St Veit Pongau |
| **Telephone** | (0043) 0676 7497550 |
| **Email** | friesenberghaus@sbg.at |
| **Website** | www.friesenberghaus.at |

Named after the historic German town of
Friesenberg, Friesenberg Haus is a very pleasant,
traditional three-storey stone-built hut that has the
honour of being the highest hut in the Zillertal at
just under 2500m. Not surprisingly the hut has a
commanding view over the main peaks of the
Zillertal and Zamsergrund valley.

The hut has a very interesting, if somewhat
tragic, history. The hut was built in 1921 as a private enterprise by the Jewish community and sub-
sequently enlarged between 1928 and 1930. Then, as dark clouds passed over
Europe, in 1938 the Jewish Huettenwirt was in the unenviable position of warden-
ing the hut at a time when the hut and its environs were being used to train the
very best of the German army's Wehrmacht elite mountain troops.

A plaque in the hallway commemorates the assistance of Jewish climbers
during the pre-war period and states: 'In the memory of the Jewish climbers and
their friends who between 1923 and 1930 built the Friesenberg Haus. In 1968
it was handed over by the survivors to the Berlin Sektion of the DAV, as thanks
for their resistance against the expulsion of Jewish climbers in 1933 from the
DAV and OeAV.' In 1980 Sektion Berlin presented the plaque to the surviving
150 members of the Donau Mountaineering Club to celebrate 50 years of the
Friesenberg Haus.

Unfortunately, after the Second World War attempts to warden the hut proved
too difficult and the hut was abandoned; soon, without care, it fell into a state
of dereliction. The hut was then adopted by the Schmitt family from Heidelberg,
who took possession and rented the hut in about 1964. With lots of hard work and
care, they gradually restored the hut into its present condition. They should have
our unconditional thanks for having been such exemplary custodians of such a
splendid place.

Just outside the hut is a bronze plaque mounted on a natural stone column
that was presented by the DAV in 2001 to celebrate 80 years of the Friesenberg
Haus, with a proclamation against 'intolerance and hate'.

## DAY WALK FROM MAYRHOFEN

**Bus service from Mayrhofen**
**Outward**    09.15/10.15 to the terminus at Schlegeisspeicher reservoir
**Return**     15.55/16.55/17.55

From the restaurant at the Schlegeis bus terminus, walk down the road in the direction of Mayrhofen for a short distance to a signpost indicating the way to Dominikus Hut and Friesenberg Haus. Pick up the trail and follow Route 532 generally in a northerly direction first through the forest and scrub vegetation, and after a short hour the farm building for storing hay at Friesenberg Alm is reached (a pleasant place for a short break). The route now cranks up a few degrees and follows a good but rocky path through the hanging valley below the steep rocky slopes of Gamsleiten. Midway, the Lapenkarbach stream is crossed, which is followed by a gradually steepening series of zigzags that traverses across the slopes under the Friesenberg Haus on the 2300m contour. A further short distance to round a corner and the hut reveals itself (3hrs).

## FURTSCHAGL HAUS (2295M)

| | |
|---|---|
| **Owner** | DAV Sektion Berlin |
| **Location** | On the southwest flank of the Grosser Moseler, with spectacular mountain scenery and a stunning view of the Hochfeiler |
| **Open** | Mid-June to end of September |
| **Facilities** | 120M/12N Good restaurant and toilet facilities; token-operated showers |
| **Connections** | From Mayrhofen via Schlegeis, Breitlahner and Ginzling (bus from Mayrhofen 09.15/10.15/11.40/13.25; from Schlegeis 10.20/12.00/13.55/15.55/16.55/17.55). Olperer Hut 5–6hrs, Berliner Hut 6hrs, Pfitscherjoch Haus 4–5hrs |
| **Address** | Frau Barbara Gratz, Dornauberg Nr 123, A-6295 Ginzling Zillertal |
| **Telephone** | (0043) 0676 9579818 |
| **Email** | furtschaglhaus@a1.net |
| **Website** | www.furtschaglhaus.com |

The hut occupies a commanding setting, with wall-to-wall mountain scenery among some of the Zillertal's finest mountains, including the Zillertal's first and second highest peaks, the Hochfeiler (3510m) and Grosser Moseler (3480m) respectively. It goes without saying that there are no easy routes on these mountains. Aspirant alpinists may ponder from the hut's terrace an ascent of the Hochfeiler's classic 500m high Norwand north face, first climbed over three days in 1887 now rarely climbed except in winter.

The hut was constructed in 1889 and opened with just 20 beds and a small room for ladies. The hut was extended in 1893 and 1912, then remained virtually unchanged for almost 50 years, except for the addition of electricity and modern plumbing. The hut was enlarged in 1968 and again in 1990 into its present size, and then for the 2000 millennium celebrations it had a cosmetic makeover with a refurbished dormitory, Gaste Stube, kitchen and washrooms.

## DAY WALK FROM MAYRHOFEN

**Bus to and from Schlegeisspeicher reservoir bus terminus**
**Outward**          (from Mayrhofen railway station) 09.15/10.15
**Return**           15.55/16.55/17.55

From the restaurant adjacent to the reservoir, with your back to Mayrhofen, walk along the road for 200m to the large car parking area where the road ends (signpost for Furtschagl Haus, Olperer Hut, Pfitscherjoch Haus). Follow Route 502 (better known as the Central Alpine Way) southeast along the shoreline of the man-made lake until it comes to a natural end (1½hrs). There are excellent retrospective views across the reservoir towards the Olperer and Hoeher Riffler, where sharp eyes will locate both the Olperer Hut and Friesenberg Haus.

Continue to follow the service track, and after a short distance a signpost points the way uphill to Furtschagl Haus. Turn northeast and follow the zigzagging trail, first through scrub vegetation followed by a rocky path, to arrive at the hut (1½hrs; 3hrs in total). Enjoy excellent views of the Hochfeiler.

# GAMS HUT (1916M)

| | |
|---|---|
| **Owner** | DAV Sektion Otterfing |
| **Location** | At the foot of the Grindberg Spitze east ridge, with a commanding view over Mayrhofen and the Zillertal valley |
| **Open** | Mid-June to end of September |
| **Facilities** | 40M/10N Excellent restaurant and toilet facilities |
| **Connections** | To Mayrhofen via Finkenberg or Ginzling (bus from Ginzling 10.10/11.10/14.30/16.10). Friesenberg Haus 8–10hrs |
| **Address** | Frau Rosemarie Gruber-Huber, Gams Huette, Oberbichl 743, A-6284 Ramsau im Zillertal |
| **Telephone** | (0043) 0676 343 7741 |
| **Email** | info@gamshuette.at |
| **Website** | www.gamshuette.at |

This hut has the distinction of being the lowest on the Zillertal Rucksack Route. Despite this lowly stature, the hut enjoys a commanding view across the Zemmgrund valley towards the peak of the Dristner, where my close friend Helmut Meier died in a fateful fall. From Mayrhofen, the hut's gleaming roof makes it clearly visible on the east ridge of Grindberg Spitze, which dominates the scene over the Zillertal valley.

The Gams is a pleasant two-storey building with a splendid copper roof, which projects a golden glow when the sun hits it from the right direction. The hut is easily accessible from Finkenberg and Ginzling, making it a popular day excursion for valley walkers, who pack the hut's terrace during the day. However, once the sun has gone down it's not unusual to have the run of the place, as the only residents will be those starting or finishing the Zillertal Rucksack Route.

The hut was built in 1927 as a private enterprise, and was known as the Grunerberg Hut. It was purchased by the DAV Sektion Kurmack from the northern German province of Prussia before being transferred after the Second World War to DAV Sektion Berlin in 1956, who in turn passed the hut to DAV Sektion Otterfing, the present owners.

Modernised and extended in 1988 the hut has two dining rooms, whose walls are liberally decorated with horns from the head of the goat-sized gamsbok mountain antelope (trophies from various hunting trips) – hence the hut's name. The original dining room also has a bar, which will be a welcome sight for many beer drinkers, particularly those celebrating the completion of the Zillertal Rucksack Route.

## DAY WALK FROM MAYRHOFEN

| Post bus to Ginzling from Mayrhofen railway station | |
|---|---|
| Outward | 09.15/10.15 |
| Return | 16.30/17.30/18.30 |

There is a choice of routes for this walk via either Finkenberg or Ginzling.

For Finkenberg, start from Mayrhofen railway station by picking up the trail of Route 12, heading north past Gasthof Clara, then turning left (west) to cross the Zillerbach river. Once across the river turn left, heading southwest upstream on Route 12 across various pasture and pleasant alpine-type meadows into the charming little village of Finkenberg. Now head more south across the picturesque gravity-defying Teufelsbruecke (Devil's Bridge) over the Zemmbach river and gorge. Thereafter, follow the steep zigzagging trail on Route 533 through the

Brunnhauswald forest to the hut (4hrs). Return by the same route or alternatively descend to the village of Ginzling.

For Ginzling, start from Mayrhofen railway station by taking the post bus to Ginzling. Get off the bus at Schrambach then, once across the Zemmbach river, head north for a short kilometre (signpost). From here head northwest, following the steep zigzagging forest trail that climbs for almost 1000m through woodland to the hut (3hrs).

## GERAER HUT (2326M)

| | |
|---|---|
| **Owner** | DAV Sektion Landshut |
| **Location** | On a level platform at the upper edge of alpine meadows overlooking the Stubai Alps, forcibly hemmed in to the rear by the sheer rock walls of the Schrammacher and Fusstein |
| **Open** | Mid-June to end of September, depending on the weather |
| **Facilities** | 80B/100M/12N Good restaurant and toilet facilities with hot water and showers. Drying room, internet facility, Seilbahn rucksack delivery service. |
| **Connections** | From Innsbruck by regional train service to Steinach am Brenner at 09.22/10.22/11.22. Then by post bus to Touristenrast guest house in the Alpeinertal valley 11.45/13.35, a journey time of around 1hr. Note that there is no bus service on Sundays. Taxi service available from Steinach railway station; 20mins ride by taxi. Olperer Hut 6–7hrs, Pfitscherjoch Haus 6–7hrs (plus 2hrs for essential diversion) |
| **Address** | Geraer Huette, Herr Arthur Lanthaler, Vals 24b/1, A-6154 St Jodok am Brenner, Austria |
| **Telephone** | (0043) 0676 9610 303 |
| **Mobile** | (0043) 0664 5106 830 |
| **Email** | office@geraerhuette.at |
| **Website** | www.geraerhuette.at |

The hut is managed by the husband-and-wife team of Arthur and Karin Lanthaler. Arthur is by profession a mountain guide, and is very helpful should you need advice about the mountains and the area in general. The hut is named after the northeast German town of Gera and occupies a commanding position high above the Valsertal valley. It has good views over the Valsertal and Wipptal valleys

towards the Stubai Alps, while to the rear the hut is hemmed in by the dominating peaks of the Schrammacher (3364m) and Fusstein (3380m).

During the Second World War the hut was occupied by German military engineers, as the area above the hut was mined for chrome molybdenum, and relics from that era lie scattered above the hut.

Built in 1895, this is a charming old, traditional two-storey hut with walls clad with larch shingles, and topped off with a bright copper roof. Internally everything is made of wood, including timber-panelled walls, boarded floors, decorative ceiling, tables, chairs, and even the water stand, all collectively providing a warm rustic charm. The creaking timbers and gentle soft furnishings all add to a very charming cosy atmosphere, making this a brilliant hut.

## GREIZER HUT (2226M)

| | |
|---|---|
| **Owner** | DAV Sektion Greiz |
| **Location** | On the western flank of the Griesfeld, with a commanding view of the Floitenkees glacier and peaks of the Schwarzenstein – this is one of the best situated huts in the Zillertal |

| | |
|---|---|
| **Open** | End of June to end of September |
| **Facilities** | 24B/52M/14N Excellent restaurant and basic (but adequate) toilet facilities that can be a little cramped when the hut is full. Drying room. |
| **Connections** | To Ginzling then post bus to Mayrhofen. Shuttle minibus/taxi service available to/from the hut's Seilbahn material goods hoist (tel Floitental Huetten Taxi 0664 1029354). Kasseler Hut 6hrs, Grune Wand Haus 6hrs, Schwarzenstein Hut 5hrs, Berliner Hut 6–8hrs |
| **Excursions** | Grosser Loeffler 5–6hrs, Schwarzenstein 6hrs |
| **Address** | Herr Herbert and Irmi Schneeberger, Oberbichl 769, A-6184 Ramsau, Zillertal |
| **Telephone** | (0043) 05282 3211 |
| **Mobile** | (0043) 0664 140 5003 |
| **Email** | greizerhuette@aon.at |
| **Website** | www.greizerhuette.at |

Constructed in 1897, and subsequently enlarged in 1905, 1927 and then again in 1972 and 1974, the hut belongs to Sektion Griez, a former Sektion of the East German DAV. It is quite an old, but superb little hut which has all the feelings of Gemutlichkeit as soon as you pass through its front door. The Alte Gastestube is adorned with the Greiz coat of arms and portraits of Huettenwirts throughout the hut's golden age.

The views from the hut terrace and dining room are as fine as any in the Alps; those looking towards the Floitenkees glacier are exceptional, with wall-to-wall mountain scenery that provides a suitable backdrop for rest and relaxation. The hut was originally built to provide easy access to the Floitenkees glacier and routes across the Schwarzenstein into the then South Tyrol. With the recession of the glacier over the years, individuals may well wonder why the hut was not built higher up! It is worth remembering that in 1900 the Floitenkees glacier was just a short 100m from the hut's front door.

This is also one of the few remaining huts that relies for its provisions on both a Seilbahn material goods hoist and the services of the Haflinger horse. These fine beasts of burden are renowned for their size and strength, having been bred over the centuries to cope with steep alpine terrain.

The winter room at the hut was added in 1926, and if you are lucky enough to get billeted in this annexe the wonderful Haflinger horses will keep you company – along with the winter room's other smaller four-pawed creatures that will enjoy foraging through your rucksack and other belongings if you forget to store your gear off the floor!

## DAY WALK FROM MAYRHOFEN

**Post bus service to Ginzling from Mayrhofen railway station**

| | |
|---|---|
| **Outward** | 09.15/10.15/11.40 |
| **Return** | 16.30/17.30/18.30 |

From Ginzling take the Floitental shuttle taxi service (tel 0664 1029354) to the Seilbahn material goods hoist at Ausserer Keesboden (this area is much used for hunting of the long-horned steinbock, better known as ibex). Thereafter follow Route 521 along a rocky track that climbs initially quite gradually, but then steepens considerably following a rocky zigzag trail to the hut (2hrs).

## HOCHFEILER HUT (2710M)

| | |
|---|---|
| **Owner** | AVS Sektion Sterzing |
| **Location** | On the southern flank of the Hochfeiler, with a level platform hewn out of the rock overlooking the Gilder Ferner glacier |
| **Open** | End of June to early October |
| **Facilities** | 31B/63M Good restaurant and toilet facilities with hot water and token-operated showers. Drying room. |
| **Connections** | There are no easy valley connections from this hut. Pfitscherjoch Haus 6–7hrs, Edelraute Hut 3hrs |
| **Excursions** | Hochfeiler 3–4hrs, Hochferner Spitze 6hrs |
| **Address** | Herr Walter Schoelzhorn, Hochfeiler Huette, I-39040 Pfitsch, Italy |
| **Telephone** | (0039) 05226 2218 or 0472 646071 |
| **Email** | office@hochfeilerhuette.it |
| **Website** | www.hochfeilerhuette.it |
| **Note** | Also known as Rifugio Gran Pilastro. This hut is very busy because of its proximity to the Hochfeiler, and you are strongly advised to reserve beds even if on your own. |

This is a high hut at just over 2700m and, not surprisingly, is a very robust three-storey stone structure built to withstand the elements. Indeed, when the hut opened the Gilder Ferner glacier passed within 100m of the hut's front door.

The original hut opened in August 1881 and was known as the Wiener Hut, being named after OeAV Sektion Vienna. In 1894 Sir Martin Conway passed this way during his Grand Traverse of the Alps. After the First World War the hut passed into Italian hands, with ownership being bestowed on CAI Section Monza in 1922. The passing years witnessed a lean time as the hut was mostly occupied by the Italian military. During the Second World War the hut was badly damaged by the American airforce, general neglect and the ravages of the weather.

With wartime damage repaired, the hut reopened in 1950, and further repairs took place throughout the decade to 1960. Along with other huts in the South Tyrol, the hut witnessed smuggling and insurgency activity across the border with Austria; this led the Italian Alpini to blow the hut up in 1962, thus forcing it to close for the next 20 years. The replacement hut opened in 1986, being built much higher up the mountain than the old hut (the original foundations are still visible below the present hut at the start of the zigzag path).

The dining room is very pleasant, with a commanding view down the Pfitschertal valley and a terrific view across the great void to the Austrian Stubai Alps. With binoculars it should be possible to locate the Becher Haus located on its rocky knoll. The dining room also displays a photographic print of a painting by the Victorian artist ET Compton of the Wiener Hut in 1900. The painting was presented to the OeAV in 1966 and is displayed in the Alpine Museum in Innsbruck.

This is a very busy hut, with most residents wanting to climb the highest peak in the Zillertal, the Hochfeiler (3510m), by its easiest of routes.

## KASSELER HUT (2177M)

| | |
|---|---|
| **Owner** | DAV Sektion Kassel |
| **Location** | At the foot of the Hinterer Stangen Spitze west ridge, with a commanding view of the Grosser Loeffler |
| **Open** | Mid-June to mid-September |
| **Facilities** | 30B/78M/10N Excellent restaurant and toilet facilities, including token-operated showers. Seilbahn rucksack delivery service; drying room, internet facility; excellent daily weather forecast in English. |

| Connections | To/from Mayrhofen via the shuttle service from Europahaus/ Grune Wand Haus (tel (0043) 05285 63423 or mobile 0664 2006 596). Karl von Edel Hut 8–10hrs, Greizer Hut 6hrs |
| Excursions | Woellbach Spitze (3209m) 4hrs, Grune Wand Spitze (2946m) 3hrs (note that a Klettersteige protected climb is likely to be established on the Grune Wand Spitze in the near future) |
| Address | Martin Gamper, Postfach 167, A-6290 Mayrhofen |
| Telephone | (0043) 0664 4016 033 |
| Email | kasseler-huette@alpenverein-kassel.de |
| Website | www.alpenverein-kassel.de |

This is a pleasant hut with a traditional timber-panelling interior. It was constructed in 1927 and subsequently enlarged in 1938, 1958 and 1982. However, the hut's true heart lies elsewhere, as the original Kasseler Hut was built in 1877 in the Riesenferner group of the South Tyrol. That hut was forfeited to Italy in 1919 after the First World War as part of war reparations and is now known as the Rifugio Vedretta di Reis.

The hut is presently wardened by brothers Martin and Marcus Gamper, who are brilliant at what they do – making visitors welcome in the Gemutlichkeit tradition and, in particular, providing the all-important reading of the daily weather forecast in English.

The hut is frequently used by various alpine schools and is often busy. Make enquiries with the hut or the Europahaus Tourist Information Centre in Mayrhofen to secure bed space.

## DAY WALK FROM MAYRHOFEN AND ALTERNATIVE TO ZRR STAGES 1–2

**Shuttle minibus service from Mayrhofen to Grune Wand Haus**

**Outward**  (from the post office and Europahaus Tourist Information Centre) 08.00/08.30/10.00/11.30/15.00

**Return**  10.00/11.30/16.00

To reserve the shuttle service tel (0043) 05285 63423 or 0664 2006 596

This day walk from Mayrhofen to the Kasseler Hut can also be used by those on the ZRR who wish to bypass the Edel Hut (Stage 1) and and go straight to the Kasseler Hut (end of Stage 2) from Mayrhofen, so avoiding the rigours of Stage 2.

Follow the route description of ZRR Stage 1 into Mayrhofen, passing the Elisabeth Hotel and moving to the post office. At the rear of the post office is a car park, from where a regular minibus service operates between Mayrhofen and Grune Wand Haus in the Stilluppgrund valley. Alternatively, make your way to the centre of Mayrhofen to Europahaus Tourist Information Centre, just 5mins walk from the railway station, to catch the minibus.

From Grune Wand Haus follow signs and paths for the Kasseler Hut. The first 1km of the trail is a continuation of the hut service road to the Seilbahn material goods hoist. Here rucksacks can be placed on the Seilbahn for a modest fee to allow a rucksack-free walk to the hut. From the Seilbahn the track heads through the Stapfenwald forest following a zigzag trail overlooking the Sonntagskarbach river and gorge. The track eventually joins up with the route and path leading to the Edel Hut on the Siebenschneidensteig ('seven ridges way') (signpost). Thereafter the route turns right and heads south over rocky broken ground to the hut (2hrs).

## KARL VON EDEL HUT (2238M)

| | |
|---|---|
| **Owner** | DAV Sektion Wurzburg |
| **Location** | Above Mayrhofen on the western slopes of the Ahorn Spitze |
| **Open** | Mid-June to end of September |
| **Facilities** | 30B/50M/41N Excellent restaurant and toilet facilities, including showers. Internet facility. |
| **Connections** | To Mayrhofen via the Ahornbahn cable car. Kasseler Hut 8–10hrs |
| **Excursions** | Ahorn Spitze 2hrs |
| **Address** | Siegfried and Gabi Schneeberger, Edel Huette, Kumbichl 873e, A-6290 Mayrhofen |
| **Telephone** | (0043) 05285 62168 |
| **Mobile** | (0043) 0664 915 4851 |
| **Email** | info@apart-schneeberger.at |
| **Website** | www.dav-wuerzburg.de |

Constructed in 1889, the hut was named after the president of the German Alpine Club in that year. The hut remained unchanged until 1951, when it was wrecked by a devastating avalanche off the Ahorn Spitze that forced it to close for the next six years. Once re-established, the hut was enlarged in 1959, refurbished in 1977, and enlarged again in 2001 to its present size.

The hut is wardened by husband-and-wife team Siegfried and Gabi Schneeberger. This is a popular day hut, being easily accessible from Mayrhofen, and many people make the short 2hr walk from the Ahornbahn cable-car station (which boasts the largest cable-car gondola in the Tyrol – akin to a double-decker bus lying flat on its side). Once at the hut these visitors spend their time either sitting on the hut's terrace or expending some more energy by making the 2hr ascent of the Ahorn Spitze (2973m). However, once the sun dips below the horizon, it is not unusual to have the run of the place – enjoy its lofty position overlooking the bright lights of Mayrhofen and the Zillertal valley.

## Day walk from Mayrhofen

See ZRR Stage 1 for the route from Mayrhofen to the Karl von Edel Hut. Allow 2hrs from the cable-car station at Filzen Alm to the hut; similarly for the return journey.

## Nevesjoch Hut (2420m)

| | |
|---|---|
| **Owner** | CAI Sektion Bolzano (Bozen) |
| **Location** | In the broad saddle of the very prominent Nevesjoch |
| **Open** | Mid-June to early October |
| **Facilities** | 31B/30M/10N Good restaurant service, but nominal toilet facilities that can feel cramped when the hut is full. However, the hut does have an excellent shower facility that would suit any hotel and is available for a modest fee. |
| **Connections** | Neves Stausee reservoir 5hrs. Edelraute Hut 4–5hrs, Schwarzenstein Hut 8–9hrs, Berliner Hut 8hrs |
| **Excursions** | Grosser Moseler (3480m) 4hrs |
| **Address** | Roland and Anna Gruber, Nevesjoch (Alte Chemnitzer) Huette, I-39032 Sand in Taufers, Italy |
| **Telephone** | (0039) 0474 653244 |
| **Email** | info@chemnitzerhuette.com |
| **Website** | www.nevesjochhuette.it |
| **Note** | Also known as Alte Chemnitzer Hut and Rifugio G Porro |

The original hut, comprising a low wooden building of just two small rooms with a roof loft, was built by the local OeAV Sektion Taufers during 1889–93, with a modest extension being added in 1895. The hut, while unwardened at the time, was being extended when Sir Martin Conway passed through in 1895 on his Grand Traverse of the Alps. He noted that his party had to share the hut with a bunch of unfriendly local workmen who were gruff and unsavoury characters, and lots of overfriendly mice.

Having no money the local Sektion Taufers sought funds from the DAV Sektion Chemnitz. Not surprisingly, when the ownership was transferred to them they renamed the hut the Chemnitzer Hut (better known today as the Alte Chemnitzer Hut), being named after north German town of Chemnitz.

The original part of the hut, no doubt where Sir Martin stayed, is the section at the front of the hut that houses the Alte Gaste Stube and first-floor bedrooms. During the First World War the hut was closed, being occupied by the Austrian military; by 1916, due to the ravages of war, Sektion Chemnitz had been reduced to just 669 members. With the loss of the South Tyrol, Sektion Chemnitz forfeited the hut, opting to build a new hut, the Neue Chemnitzer Hut, which opened in 1926 in the Piztal region of the Tyrol. That hut would also have a chequered history, with ownership passing between various DAV Sektions, eventually to DAV Sektion Russelheim in 1980–81.

Meanwhile the Alte Chemnitzer Hut had the same experience as all the other huts on the South Tyrol border with Austria up to the Second World War. The hut was bombed and destroyed by the English and American airforce, and by 1945 it was almost in ruins.

A hut of sorts was built from the materials of the original hut and managed to open in 1953. However, during the 1960s smuggling was again rife across the South Tyrol and this led to the Italian military, the Alpini, taking over the hut and staying for the next 10 years (1962–72). When the army did vacate the hut it was in a ruinous state, but it managed to reopen in 1974.

## OLPERER HUT (2389M)

| | |
|---|---|
| **Owner** | DAV Sektion Neumarkt |
| **Location** | On the lower eastern slopes of the Olperer, with a truly stunning view across the Schlegeis reservoir to the Hochfeiler and Grosser Moseler |
| **Open** | Early June to early October |
| **Facilities** | 60M/12N Good restaurant facilities and toilet facilities with token-operated showers. Drying room. |
| **Connections** | To/from Mayrhofen via Schlegeis and Breitlahner (bus from Mayrhofen 09.15/10.15/11.40; from Schlegeis 12.00/13.55/15.55/16.55/17.55). Friesensenberg Haus 3hrs, Furtschagl Haus 5hrs, Geraer Hut 6hrs, Pfitscherjoch Haus 5hrs |
| **Address** | Katrina and Manuel Daum, Dornauberg 110, A-6295 Ginzling, Zillertal |
| **Telephone** | (0043) 07203 46930 |
| **Mobile** | (0043) 0664 417 6566 |
| **Email** | info@olpererhuette.de |
| **Website** | www.olpererhuette.de |
| **Note** | The hut can get very busy, so it is advisable either to avoid the weekends or to make a reservation – even if you are travelling alone. |

This is a splendid hut, with a commanding view over the Schlegeisspeicher reservoir towards the two highest peaks in the Zillertal range – the Hochfeiler (3510m) and the Grosser Moseler (3480m). The original hut was quite small, but had an excellent rustic quality. Initially constructed in 1881 by Sektion Prague, it was soon demolished by avalanche. The hut was rebuilt in 1900 by donations from DAV Sektion Berlin, and soon afterwards it was transferred to their care. The hut was refurbished in 1931 and then modestly extended in 1976. The hut was badly damaged by a mudslide in 1998 that tore the back off the hut, forcing it to close

for a season while the debris was removed and the hut repaired. But the old hut was never to be the same again.

Change came when ownership of the hut was transferred from Sektion Berlin to the Bavarian Sektion Neumarkt in 2004. Full of vim and vigour, the new owners set about constructing the delightful Neumarkter Runde Panorama Hoehenweg route in 2006. The new owners also quickly realised that the old hut was totally inadequate for the volume of traffic coming and going on the Zillertal Rucksack Route, plus daily visitors from Mayrhofen, and it closed in 2006. The old hut was demolished and replaced by an entirely new hut that opened in 2007. This has an expanded capacity for 60 people, accommodated in 5 rooms for 4 people and 5 rooms for 8 people. The old winter room was similarly upgraded and refurbished to sleep 12.

The new hut is a move away from the traditional mountain hut design, being a simple two-storey rectangular structure with a pitched roof. Construction is of prefabricated timber panels all flown in by helicopter. Internally the hut is bright and clean, with an uncluttered ambience. The centrepiece is a full-width panoramic window overlooking the head of the Schlegeisspeicher reservoir and the fabulous peaks of the Hochfeiler and Grosser Moseler. With the construction of a road in the early 1970s (part of the Schlegeis hydro-electric project), the hut has become easily accessible from Mayrhofen, and this means at weekends it is usually a very noisy full house.

The main excursion from the hut is to climb the Olperer (3476m), third highest peak in the Zillertal, via the southeast ridge. The hut occupies an important position on the Zillertal Rucksack Route and the Olperer Runde Tour.

## DAY WALK FROM MAYRHOFEN

**Bus from Mayrhofen to the bus terminus at Schlegeis reservoir and roadside restaurant**

| | |
|---|---|
| **Outward** | 09.15/10.15/11.40 |
| **Return** | 12.00/13.55/15.55/16.55/17.55 |

From the restaurant follow one of the routes described in ZRR Stage 6. Either the direct route or the marginally longer but more scenically rewarding Neumarkter Runde Panorama Hoehenweg (3hrs). The scenic route offers excellent scenery throughout, particularly the latter part of the walk, with fabulous views across the Schlegeisspeicher reservoir towards the high peaks.

## PFITSCHERJOCH HAUS (2277M)

| | |
|---|---|
| **Owner** | Private |
| **Location** | On the Italian southwest side of the Pfitscherjoch, about 500m from the Austrian border |
| **Open** | Late June to end of September |
| **Facilities** | 30B/100M/12N Excellent restaurant and toilet facilities |
| **Connections** | To Schlegeis Stausee reservoir (2+hrs), then by post bus to Mayrhofen 10.20/12.00/13.35/15.55/16.55/17.55. Geraer Hut 6–7hrs, Olperer Hut 6hrs, Hochfeiler Hut 6–7hrs |
| **Address** | Josef Volgger, Pfitscherjoch Haus, Wiesen 138a, I-39040 Pfitsch, Italy |
| **Telephone** | (0039) 0472 630119 |
| **Email** | volgger-josef@rolmail.net |
| **Website** | www.pfitscherjochhaus.com |
| **Note** | Also known as Rifugio Passo Vizze |

This superbly sited hut was built in 1884 by Alois Rainer, a hotelier from St Jakob in Pfitsch. The hut was rebuilt in 1969, extended in 1982 and modernised in 2000, and has excellent facilities, as would be expected of a hotel.

During the First World War, the hut was garrisoned by the Austrian army until the armistice of 1918, when the whole of the South Tyrol was forfeited to Italy. From 1919 the hut was garrisoned by the alpine troops of the Italian army, including the elite Alpini. Fearing an invasion by the Austrians to claim back the South Tyrol the Italians fortified the area to the extent that remnants of barrack buildings still exist just below the hut, along with signs of the extensive trench systems that can still be seen today (albeit overgrown). After the war, the military of both sides maintained an uneasy presence on the Joch (pass) to prevent counterinsurgency and the smuggling of goods, which was rife. Life in Austria after the First World War was grim. Indeed, Frank Smythe in his book *Over Tyrolese Hills* commented how sad he was to see such fortifications in the mountains.

This situation would last until the Second World War, when there was a friendly truce of sorts. However, after the war both sides resorted to their pre-1938 positions, the Austrians wanting the South Tyrol back and the Italians resisting such concessions. This pertained for the next 20 years, until in 1966 the Italian army decided their only option was to blow the hut up. A further five years would pass before normal border crossings were allowed.

Following the destruction of the hut and the vacation of the military from Pfitscherjoch, the hut was eventually given back to its rightful owners, who then had the daunting task of suing for compensation. Many years would again pass before the hut could be rebuilt, and it eventually reopened in 1980. Pfitscherjoch Haus is a big hut that caters for all mountain travellers, particularly trans-Alp cyclists. The main Gaste Stube is self-service, with all sorts of meals on offer. The hut has dormitory Matratzenlager rooms, but also proper bedrooms with en-suite facilities. While this is a big hut, it is quite pleasant for a short stay.

## SCHWARZENSTEIN HUT (2922M)

| | |
|---|---|
| **Owner** | CAI Sektion Brunneck |
| **Location** | On a level rock promontory on the southern Italian side of the Tribbachschneide ridge |
| **Open** | Mid-June to end of September |
| **Facilities** | 45B Excellent restaurant service, limited but adequate toilet facilities due to its location and height |

| | |
|---|---|
| **Connections** | There are no easy valley or hut connections from this hut. To Luttach in the Rotbachtal valley 5hrs, Nevesjoch Hut 8–10hrs, Berliner Hut via Schwarzenstein 7–8hrs, Greizer Hut via Floitenkees glacier 5hrs |
| **Excursions** | Schwarzenstein 3hrs, Floiten Spitze 2hrs |
| **Address** | Herr Guenther Knapp, Stagackerfeld 6, I-39030 St Johann, Sud Tyrol, Italy |
| **Telephone** | (0039) 04734 671160 or 676219 |
| **Email** | info@schwarzensteihuette.com |
| **Website** | www.schwarzenstein.com |
| **Note** | Also known as Rifugio Vittorio Veneto al Sasso Nero |

This very plain-looking hut is in the top drawer of alpine huts, being recognised by the European Union as a building of historical importance due to its location overlooking the Rieserferner mountains and peaks of the Sexten Dolomites. More recently, the hut was the first in the Alps to have an internet home page and a live-view webcam. Having to withstand savage and severe weather, the hut is a very stout and robust building. Built in 1895 by the D&OeAV Sektion Leipzig, the hut opened with spaces for just 16 people. At this time the adjacent glacier systems passed equidistant on both sides of the hut and Tribbachschneide ridge. The hut was enlarged in 1896 to its present size and has remained virtually unchanged since 1914 apart from the addition of modern plumbing and electricity.

As with the other huts along the South Tyrol everything was fine until the start of the First World War, when from 1914 to 1927 the hut was closed. After Austria's loss of the South Tyrol and the treaty of St Germain in September 1919, the hut was taken over by the Italian military before being transferred to the Italian Alpine Club and Sektion Vittorio Veneto, who reopened it in July 1927. The hut struggled to survive due to the political antagonism between Austria and Italy, with both armies being camped out on the icy wastes of the Schwarzensteinsattel (saddle) – a situation that would simply not go away.

During the Second World War the hut was used to train alpine troops and struggled to survive until it was forced to close from 1943 to 1948. When it did reopen temporarily the hut, like others in the South Tyrol, was a semi-wreck and unfit for use, having been plundered for its doors, windows and anything else that could be carried away.

Unfortunately the hut is now beginning to suffer structural failure due to the gradual melting of the permafrost that holds together all the friable rocks on which it sits. The EU have agreed that because of the hut's historical significance it should be demolished and a new hut built slightly higher up the Tribbachschneide

189

ridge. Despite the pledge to fund the project, there are no signs of the money materialising from the EU.

Gunther Knapp, who has been the guardian for the past 35 years and is a teacher by profession, is often seen with construction materials trying against all odds to stop the hut from falling down. Gunther's other main attribute is that he is a master 'Schnappsetier' (maker of Schnapps) and Gaste Stube entertainer in the ways of the Alte Sud Tyrol, which makes this a very welcoming hut!

# APPENDIX A
*Route summary tables*

| | | | ZILLERTAL RUCKSACK ROUTE | | | |
|---|---|---|---|---|---|---|
| **Stage** | **Start** | **Finish** | **Distance** | **Ascent** | **Time** | |
| Stage 1 | Mayrhofen | Karl von Edel Hut | 3km | 283m | 3hrs | |
| Stage 2 | Karl von Edel Hut | Kasseler Hut | 14km | 800m (750m descent) | 8–10hrs | |
| Stage 3 | Kasseler Hut | Greizer Hut | 7.5km | 700m | 6–7hrs | |
| Stage 4 | Greizer Hut | Berliner Hut | 8km | 1220m | 6–8hrs | |
| Stage 4a | Greizer Hut | Berliner Hut | 10km; 12km via the Schwarzenstein Hut | 1100m; 1115m via the Schwarzenstein Hut | 6hrs; 10hrs via the Schwarzenstein Hut | |
| Stage 5 | Berliner Hut | Furtschagl Haus | 8km | 1041m | 6–7hrs | |
| Stage 6 | Furtschagl Haus | Olperer Hut | 9km | 590m | 5–6hrs | |
| Stage 6a | Furtschagl Haus | Olperer Hut | 12.5km | 480m | 10–11hrs | |
| Stage 7 | Olperer Hut | Friesenberg Haus | 4km | 580m | 2½hrs | |
| Stage 8 | Friesenberg Haus | Gams Hut | 13km | c:1000m | 10–12hrs | |
| Stage 9 | Gams Hut | Mayrhofen | 4km to Ginzling; 3km to Finkenberg | None | 3hrs to Ginzling; 2hrs to Finkenberg | |
| | | **Total Distance** | 69.5km–78km | | | |

# APPENDIX A
*Route summary tables (continued)*

## ZILLERTAL SOUTH TYROL TOUR

| Stage | Start | Finish | Distance | Ascent | Time |
|---|---|---|---|---|---|
| Stage 1 | Touristenraste | Geraer Hut | 5km | 800m | 3–4hrs |
| Stage 2 | Geraer Hut | Pfitscherjoch Haus | 10km | c1300m | 6–7hrs |
| Stage 3 | Pfitscherjoch Haus | Hochfeiler Hut | 8km | 900m | 6–7hrs |
| Stage 4 | Hochfeiler Hut | Edelraute Hut | 4km | 250m | 3hrs |
| Stage 5 | Edelraute Hut | Nevesjoch Hut | 7km | c200m | 3hrs with a footbridge; otherwise 5hrs |
| Stage 6 | Nevesjoch Hut | Schwarzenstein Hut | 11km | c1350m (1060m descent) | 8–10 hrs |
| Stage 7 | Schwarzenstein Hut | Berliner Hut or Greizer Hut | Berliner Hut 8km; Greizer Hut 4km | Berliner Hut 315m; Greizer Hut 110m | Berliner Hut 6hrs; Greizer Hut 3–4hrs |
| Stage 6a | Furtschagl Haus | Olperer Hut | 12.5km | 480m | 10–11hrs |
| Stage 7 | Olperer Hut | Friesenberg Haus | 4km | 580m | 2½hrs |
| Stage 8 | Friesenberg Haus | Gams Hut | 13km | c1000m | 10–12hrs |
| Stage 9 | Gams Hut | Mayrhofen | 4km to Ginzling; 3km to Finkenberg | None | 3hrs to Ginzling; 2hrs to Finkenberg |
| | | **Total Distance** | 49km–53km | | |

# APPENDIX B

*Further information*

## Public transport

### Airlines

For readers based in the UK, a website such as 'Travel supermarket' will find any number of flights from the UK to Munich, Innsbruck or Salzburg from sites including the following
www.klm.com
www.bmibaby.com
www.austrianairlines.com
www.britishairways.com
www.thomsonfly.com
www.easyjet.com
www.ryanair.com
www.airlingus.com
www.lufthansa.com
www.flyniki.com

### Railways

GERMAN RAILWAYS
Deutsche Bundesbahn (DB)
www.bahn.de

AUSTRIAN RAILWAYS
Oesterreichische Bundesbahnen (OBB)
www.oebb.at

ZILLERTAL RAILWAY
Zillertalbahn
www.zillertalbahn.at

TYROL RAILWAY
Verkehrsverbund Tirol
www.vvt.at

### Bus services
Post bus
www.postbus.at

### Taxi services
Taxi Thaler
(0043) 05285 63423 or
(0043) 0664 2006596

Taxi Kroll
(0043) 05285 62967

Floitentaxi
(0043) 664 102 9354

### Information services

### Austrian National Tourist Office
Tel: (UK) 0845 1011 818
(Ireland) 189 0930 118
Fax: 020 7440 3848
Email: info.austria.info
www.holiday@austria.info

### Austrian Alpine Club (UK)
12a North Street
Wareham
Dorset BH20 4AG
Tel: 01929 556870
Fax: 01929 554729
Email: aac.office@aacuk.org.uk
www.aacuk.org.uk

## Austrian Alpine Club Head Office
Oesterreichischer Alpenverein
Olympia Strasse
A 6020 Innsbruck
Austria
Tel: 0043 (0) 512 595
Email: office@alpenverein
www.alpenverein.at

## Mayrhofen Tourist Information Centre
Europahaus Congress Centre
Durster Strasse 225
A6290 Mayrhofen
Austria
Tel: 0043 5285 6760
Email: congress@europahaus.at
www.europahaus.at
See also www.mayrhofen.at and
www.naturpark.zillertal@alpenverein.at

## Places to stay

INNSBRUCK
### The Alte Pradl Hotel
Located 10mins walk from the railway
station and 20mins from the old town.
Very quiet.
Tel: 0043 (0) 5123 45156
Email: info@hotelaltpradl.at
www.altpradl-hotel.at

### Weisses Kreuz (The White Cross)
A touch of the old and medieval
Innsbruck, located in the heart of the
Old Town. Its claim to fame is that
Mozart stayed there while playing for
the Royal Court at the Hofburg Palace.
Tel: 0043 (0) 5125 94790
Email: hotel@weisseskreuz.at
www.weisseskreuz.at

### The Goldene Krone
Located on Maria Theresien Strasse near
the triumphant arch.
Tel: 0043 (0)51258 6160
Email: info@goldene-krone.at
www.goldene-krone.at

### Nepomuks Backpackers Hostel
Located just off the main square, in
the old part of the Alte Stadt above the
Konditorei cake shop.
Tel: 0043 (0) 664 7879197 or 0043 (0)
512 584118
Email: mail@nepomuks.at
www.nepomuks.at

### Verein Volkshaus Innsbruck (youth
hostel)
Redetzky Strasse
A-6020 Innsbruck
Tel: (0043) 0664 2667004 or (0043)
0512 341086
Email: jgh.volkshaus-ibk@aon.at
www.jgh.volkshaus-ibk.at

SALZBURG
### The Zur Post Hotel
Located 5mins from the airport and
15mins walk from the centre of this fine
old city.
Tel: 0043 (0) 662 832339
Email: hotelzurpost@EUnet.at

STEINACH AM BRENNER
### The Zur Rose Hotel
Located on the main street, just 10mins
walk from the railway station, managed
by the Holzman family, with master
chef Franz providing an excellent
choice of menu.
Tel: 0043 (0) 5272 6221
Email: info@hotelrose.at
www.hotelrose.at

## Hut information

For a searchable directory of mountain huts, with links to emails and websites where available
www.bergsteigen.at/de and click on 'Hutten'
www.alpenverein.at and click on 'Hutteninfos'

## Professional mountain guides (Bergfuehrer)

The services of a professional mountain guide can be hired direct through the UK Section of the Austrian Alpine Club (UK) and the Alpenverein Akademie in Innsbruck – see www.alpenverein-akademie.at – or in Mayrhoen via Peter Habeler's Office – see www.bergfuehrer-zillertal.at.

## Guide contacts

Harry Holl
Email: team-alpin-austria@aon.at

Hannes Wettstein
Email: cmeighoernewr@t-online.de

Dougal Tavener
Email: dougal@dougaltavener.com

Marcus Moosberger
Email: info@mitmoses.at

Robert Thaler
Email: mail@alpinprofi.at

Peter Weber
Email: bergerlebnis@edumail.at

Stefan Wierer
Email: info@bergfuehrer-zillertal.at

British Association of International Mountain Leaders – see www.baiml.org

# APPENDIX C
*German–English glossary*

| German | English |
|---|---|

## Mountain terminology

| German | English |
|---|---|
| *Tal* | Valley |
| *Gletscher/Kees* | Glacier |
| *Randkluft/Spalten* | Bergschrund/Crevasses |
| *Eis* | Ice |
| *Bach/Wasserfal* | River/Stream/Waterfall |
| *See/Lac* | Tarn/Lake |
| *Wald/Baum* | Forest/Tree |
| *Alm* | Alpine hut/Pastures |
| *Weg* | Way/Footpath |
| *Berg* | Mountain |
| *Band/Grat/Kamm* | Ledge/Ridge |
| *Nadel* | Needle/Pinnacle |
| *Gipfel/Spitze* | Summit |
| *Wilde/Aperer* | Snow peak/Rock peak |
| *Scharte/Sattel/Torl* | Col/Saddle/Pass/Gate |
| *Kessel/Grube/Kar* | Couloir/Basin/Combe |
| *Nord/Sud/Ost/West* | North/South/East/West |
| *Links/Rechts/Geradeaus* | Left/Right/Straight ahead |
| *Uber/Unter* | Over/Under |
| *Hinter/Mittler/Vorder* | Further/Middle/Nearer |
| *Inner/Ausser* | Inner/Outer |
| *Wanderkarte* | Map |
| *Steinslag* | Stone fall |
| *Schweirig/Leicht* | Difficult/Easy |
| *Gefahrlich* | Dangerous |
| *Alpenvereins* | Alpine Club |
| *Bergfuehrer* | Mountain guide |
| *Nur fur geubte* | Only for the experienced |
| *Gesprutt* | Route is closed/barred |
| *Bergrettung* | Mountain rescue |
| *Kabel/Pickle* | Rope/Ice-axe |

## When travelling

| German | English |
|---|---|
| *Flughafen* | Airport |
| *Ankunft/Abflug/Abfahrt* | Arrivals/Departures |
| *Hauptbahnhof* | Railway station |
| *Gleis/Bahnsteig* | Platform |
| *Auskunft* | Information Office |
| *Ausgang/Eingang* | Exit/Entrance |
| *Platz-Reservierung* | Booking office |
| *Fahrkarten Schalter* | Ticket office |
| *Einfach* | One way/Single |

| German | English |
|---|---|
| *Ruckfahrkarte/Hin und Zuruck* | Roundtrip/Return |
| *Bushaltestelle* | Bus stop |
| *Ich moechte* | I would like |
| *Wo ist?* | Where is? |
| *Ich suche* | I'm looking for |

## When eating
### Selected menu list

| | |
|---|---|
| *Mittagessen* | Lunch |
| *Abendessen* | Evening meal |
| *Wiener Schnitzel* | Breaded veal/Pork fillets |
| *Jager Schnitzel* | Veal/Pork fillets with mushroom topping |
| *Tyroler Grotzl* | Fried potato and eggs |
| *Spiegeleier und Schinken* | Fried eggs and bacon |
| *Gulash* | Cubes of beef in a rich sauce |
| *Zweibelrostbraten* | Broiled or fried beef with onions |
| *Wurst Brot* | Sausage and bread |
| *Kase Brot* | Cheese and bread |
| *Schinken Brot* | Ham and bread |
| *Tagesuppe* | Soup of the day |
| *Knodelsuppe* | Soup with dumplings |
| *Wurstsuppe* | Soup with sausages |
| *Kaiserschmarren* | Sweet pancakes |
| *Apfelstrudel* | Apple pie |
| *Compote* | Fresh or tinned fruit |
| *Bergsteigeressen* | Climbers' meal at low cost |

### Standard accompaniments

| | |
|---|---|
| *Brot/Brotchen* | Bread/Bread rolls |
| *Kartoffeln* | Potato |
| *Gemuse* | Vegetables |
| *Reis* | Rice |
| *Salt* | Salt |
| *Pfeffer* | Pepper |
| *Senf* | Mustard |

### Vegetarian (Vegetarische) meals

| | |
|---|---|
| *Kasspatzle* | Cheese with nuddels (noodles/pasta) |
| *Kartoffel-gaertreide-bratlinge mit salat garniture* | Pan-fried potatoes with salad garnish |
| *Kartoffel mit spiegeleier* | Pan-fried potatoes with fried egg |
| *Gemischter salat* | Mixed salad |
| *Gruner salat* | Green salad |

### Other useful food-related words

| | |
|---|---|
| *Speisekarte* | Menu |
| *Tasse* | Cup |
| *Teller* | Plate |
| *Schussel* | Bowl |
| *Messer* | Knife |

Berliner Hut

| German | English |
|--------|---------|
| *Gabel* | Fork |
| *Loffel* | Spoon |
| *Messer* | Knife |
| *Bier* | Beer |
| *Weiss/Rot Wein* | White/Red wine |
| *Schnapps* | Clear, strong alcoholic spirit |
| *Tee/Café/Milch* | Tea/ Coffee/Milk |
| *Zitronen* | Lemonade |
| *Heiss/Kalt* | Hot/Cold |
| *Gross/Klein* | Large/Small |
| *Viertel/Halb* | Quarter/Half (Note drinks are served in proportions and quantities of a litre) |

| English | German |
|---------|--------|

### When ordering or paying

| English | German |
|---------|--------|
| *Excuse me* | Wie bitte |
| *Do you speak English?* | Sprechen sie Englisch? |
| *How much?/My bill, please* | Wieviel?/Mein Zahlen bitte |
| *The bill, please* | Die Rechnung bitte |
| *Can I have...* | Kann ich haben... |
| *Have you got?* | Haben sie? |
| *Have you any vegetarian options?* | Haben a vegetarische Gerichte Essen |

# APPENDIX D
*Further reading*

## Hut directory
*Alpenvereinshuetten Directory* (previously the 'Green book') *Volume 1 Ostalpen: Deutschland, Osterreich, Sudtyrol*. OeAV, AVS and DAV Bergverlag. Published by Rother. See www.rother.de

## Maps and guidebooks

### Maps
The following maps are required for both the Zillertal Rucksack Route and Zillertal South Tyrol Tour. The maps are published by the Austrian Alpine Club and are available from the UK Section of the Austrian Alpine Club (UK).

*Alpenvereinskarte Zillertal Alpen*
  Sheet 35/1 Westliches (West) 1:25,000
  Sheet 35/2 Mittler (Central) 1:25,000

The following maps are also recommended, since they cover the complete region at a glance and are available from major map retailers:

Freytag & Berndt Wanderkarte: Sheet 152 (1:50,000), *Mayrhofen, Zillertal Alpen, Gerlos-Krimml*

Kompass Wanderkarte: Sheet 37 (1:50,000), *Zillertaler Alpen; Tuxer Alpen*

## Books
*Eastern Alps: the classic routes on the highest peaks*, Dieter Seibert: Diadem Books. Includes the Hochfeiler, Grosser Loeffler, Grosser Moseler, Olperer and Schwarzenstein.

*Zillertal Alpen. 50 selected walks*: Rother Wander Fuehrer

*Trekking in the Alps*, Kev Reynolds: Cicerone Press

## Websites
These websites are mostly in German, but will no doubt eventually be translated into English.
www.zillertal.at
www.berlinerhoehenweg.at
www.naturpark.zillertal@alpenverein.at

## Inspirational reading
You may find the following mountaineering books by mountain-lovers of the past interesting and inspiring – that is, if you can track them down!

*Over Tyrolese hills*, Frank Smythe: Hodder and Stoughton (1936)

*The Alps from end to end*, Sir Martin Conway: Nelson Books (1894)

*Pictures in Tyrol and elsewhere*, Francis Fox Tuckett: Longmans, Green and Co (1867)

# INDEX

# LISTING OF CICERONE GUIDES

The Southern Fells
The Western Fells
Roads and Tracks of the Lake District
Rocky Rambler's Wild Walks
Scrambles in the Lake District North & South
Short Walks in Lakeland
  1 South Lakeland
  2 North Lakeland
  3 West Lakeland
The Cumbria Coastal Way
The Cumbria Way and the Allerdale Ramble
The Lake District Anglers' Guide
Tour of the Lake District

## DERBYSHIRE, PEAK DISTRICT AND MIDLANDS

High Peak Walks
The Star Family Walks
Walking in Derbyshire
White Peak Walks
  The Northern Dales
  The Southern Dales

## SOUTHERN ENGLAND

A Walker's Guide to the Isle of Wight
London – The definitive walking guide
The Cotswold Way
The Greater Ridgeway
The Lea Valley Walk
The North Downs Way
The South Downs Way
The South West Coast Path
The Thames Path
Walking in Bedfordshire
Walking in Berkshire
Walking in Kent
Walking in Sussex
Walking in the Isles of Scilly
Walking in the Thames Valley
Walking on Dartmoor
Walking on Guernsey
Walking on Jersey
Walks in the South Downs National Park

## WALES AND WELSH BORDERS

Backpacker's Britain – Wales
Glyndwr's Way
Great Mountain Days in Snowdonia
Hillwalking in Snowdonia
Hillwalking in Wales Vols 1 & 2
Offa's Dyke Path
Ridges of Snowdonia
Scrambles in Snowdonia
The Ascent of Snowdon
The Lleyn Peninsula Coastal Path
The Pembrokeshire Coastal Path
The Shropshire Hills
The Spirit Paths of Wales
The Wye Valley Walk
Walking in Pembrokeshire
Walking on the Brecon Beacons
Welsh Winter Climbs

## INTERNATIONAL CHALLENGES, COLLECTIONS AND ACTIVITIES

Canyoning
Europe's High Points

## EUROPEAN CYCLING

Cycle Touring in France
Cycle Touring in Ireland
Cycle Touring in Spain
Cycle Touring in Switzerland
Cycling in the French Alps
Cycling the Canal du Midi
Cycling the River Loire
The Danube Cycleway
The Grand Traverse of the Massif Central
The Way of St James

## AFRICA

Climbing in the Moroccan Anti-Atlas
Kilimanjaro: A Complete Trekker's Guide
Mountaineering in the Moroccan High Atlas
Trekking in the Atlas Mountains
Walking in the Drakensberg

## ALPS – CROSS-BORDER ROUTES

100 Hut Walks in the Alps
Across the Eastern Alps: E5
Alpine Ski Mountaineering
  1 Western Alps
  2 Central and Eastern Alps
Chamonix to Zermatt
Snowshoeing
Tour of Mont Blanc
Tour of Monte Rosa
Tour of the Matterhorn
Trekking in the Alps
Walking in the Alps
Walks and Treks in the Maritime Alps

## PYRENEES AND FRANCE/ SPAIN CROSS-BORDER ROUTES

Rock Climbs in The Pyrenees
The GR10 Trail
The Mountains of Andorra
The Pyrenean Haute Route
The Pyrenees
The Way of St James France & Spain
Through the Spanish Pyrenees: GR11
Walks and Climbs in the Pyrenees

## AUSTRIA

Trekking in Austria's Hohe Tauern
Trekking in the Stubai Alps
Trekking in the Zillertal Alps
Walking in Austria

## EASTERN EUROPE

The High Tatras
The Mountains of Romania
Walking in Bulgaria's National Parks
Walking in Hungary

## FRANCE

Ecrins National Park
GR20: Corsica
Mont Blanc Walks
Mountain Adventures in the Maurienne
The Cathar Way

_TREKKING IN THE ZILLERTAL HUT STAMPS_
ZILLERTAL RUCKSACK ROUTE (BERLINER HOEHENWEG)

| Karl von Edel Hut | Kasseler Hut | Greizer Hut |
| --- | --- | --- |
| Berliner Hut | Furtschagl Haus | Olperer Hut |
| Friesenberg Haus | Gams Hut | |

## TREKKING IN THE ZILLERTAL HUT STAMPS
### ZILLERTAL SOUTH TYROL TOUR

| Geraer Hut | Pfitscherjoch Haus | Hochfeiler Hut |
|---|---|---|
| Edelraute Hut | Nevesjoch Hut | Schwarzenstein Hut |

## Walking – Trekking – Mountaineering – Climbing – Cycling

**Over 40 years, Cicerone have built up an outstanding collection of 300 guides, inspiring all sorts of amazing adventures.**

Every guide comes from extensive exploration and research by our expert authors, all with a passion for their subjects. They are frequently praised, endorsed and used by clubs, instructors and outdoor organisations.

All our titles can now be bought as **e-books** and many as iPad and Kindle files and we will continue to make all our guides available for these and many other devices.

Our website shows any **new information** we've received since a book was published. Please do let us know if you find anything has changed, so that we can pass on the latest details. On our **website** you'll also find some great ideas and lots of information, including sample chapters, contents lists, reviews, articles and a photo gallery.

It's easy to keep in touch with what's going on at Cicerone, by getting our monthly **free e-newsletter**, which is full of offers, competitions, up-to-date information and topical articles. You can subscribe on our home page and also follow us on **Facebook** and **Twitter**, as well as our **blog**.

**Cicerone – the very best guides for exploring the world.**

## CICERONE

2 Police Square  Milnthorpe  Cumbria  LA7 7PY
Tel: 015395 62069  info@cicerone.co.uk
**www.cicerone.co.uk**